FOREWORD BY DALLAS JENKINS

THE

Redisc ~~THE CHOSEN~~
SEASON ONE

FORGOTTEN

TEACHINGS

OF JESUS

Brandon Robbins

DAVID **C** COOK®

transforming lives together

THE FORGOTTEN TEACHINGS OF JESUS:
REDISCOVERING THE BIBLE WITH THE CHOSEN: SEASON ONE
Published by David C Cook
4050 Lee Vance Drive
Colorado Springs, CO 80918 U.S.A.

Integrity Music Limited, a Division of David C Cook
Brighton, East Sussex BN1 2RE, England

DAVID C COOK˙ and related marks are registered trademarks of David C Cook.

The website addresses recommended throughout this book are offered as a resource
to you. These websites are not intended in any way to be or imply an endorsement
on the part of David C Cook, nor do we vouch for their content.

Library of Congress Control Number 2024939745
ISBN 978-0-8307-8720-3
eISBN 978-0-8307-8721-0

The Team: Michael Covington, Jeff Gerke, Gina Pottenger, Renée Chavez, Susan Murdock
Cover Design: Micah Kandros

Printed in the United States of America
First Edition 2025

1 2 3 4 5 6 7 8 9 10

101424

In loving memory of my grandfather Lloyd Butler Jr.
Never will I forget those Sundays sitting beside
you in church, the prayer breakfasts on Thursday
mornings, or the countless conversations when
you told me about your love of Jesus.
Your faith was contagious. And I caught it.

CONTENTS

FOREWORD

The Chosen is just a show.

I know, I know, you might think that sounds dismissive. When my wife Amanda or I say that, sometimes some folks get offended, thinking we're minimizing the role it has played in their lives.

To be clear, I understand the importance of tools like *The Chosen* or any piece of media in opening the door toward understanding Jesus or the Bible more. All of us have stories of a song or movie or show or book illuminating Truths we didn't otherwise fully grasp. Believe me, I'm aware of the great weight and I responsibility I have to steward this project that people all over the world tell me has drawn them closer to Jesus.

But it's still just a show. It's not the end game. Discipleship, particularly biblical discipleship, is the end game. I hope that through *The Chosen*, you might know and love Jesus more and see him more clearly, but that's only for the purpose of getting to the next step.

And that's where I hand off the baton to guys like Pastor Brandon and books like this. What Brandon has been doing masterfully on YouTube for several years is exactly what I hoped for—taking *Chosen* viewers deeper into the Scriptures and a more comprehensive understanding of the historical, theological, and biblical context of these stories.

This book is an even better and fuller version of what I've seen countless times in his videos. Yes, he's taking you deeper into the first season of *The Chosen*, but remember, it's just a show. More importantly, he's illuminating the timeless truths of the Bible and, I promise you, teaching you something new. I've learned from Brandon, and it's made *The Chosen* better. It's also helped me see familiar stories in a deeper way.

You've heard enough from me. Now pursue God and his Word more fully. Brandon, the baton is yours, and Dear Reader, you are about to grow.

Dallas Jenkins
Creator, *The Chosen*

PREFACE

The Chosen is not Scripture. I know you know this. The makers of
The Chosen themselves frequently remind their audience of this.
Nevertheless, it is something we must always remember.

The Chosen is a television show—a multi-season, crowd-funded
dramatic depiction of the life of Jesus and his disciples. It has capti-
vated people around the world and forever changed the landscape of
Christian media. It is being translated into six hundred languages, has
spawned books and Bible studies, and continues to draw generations of
people together to talk about the Gospels.

But it is not Scripture.

One of *The Chosen*'s greatest strengths is its ability to draw its
audience into the biblical story. We feel as if we are there, walking
with Jesus, one among his disciples. This is part of what has effected
such tremendous spiritual transformation in people's lives. But this
feeling can also be dangerous. Sometimes we can mistake the events
of the show for the events of Scripture; we can lose track of what
is fact and what is fiction. It may become difficult to tell what is a
storyline created by the writers, which Scriptures have been altered

to make for better television, and what is a truly accurate portrayal of the events of the Bible.

This book will help to unblur those lines.

Over the course of thirty-two chapters, we are going to dive deep into the events of the first season of the show. But more importantly, we are going to be focusing on how those events are conveyed in Scripture and how they reflect the realities of the world of Jesus. My goal for you when you read the final page of this book isn't just for you to feel like you understand the series better—I want you to understand the Bible better.

So, we won't spend a lot of time focusing on character development or the unfolding narrative of the show. Instead, we're going to look at where those events intersect with Scripture, how they reflect life at the time of Jesus, and how each of these intersections can transform the way we read the Bible.

So, as you read this book, have your Bible on hand. Study the Scriptures referenced and look for the details highlighted. May you find that the things you learn not only enhance your enjoyment of the series but draw you deeper into God's Word.

INTRODUCTION

When I was ten, my dad and I went Christmas shopping to get gifts for my cousins. They lived in a different state, and I saw them only every few years, so selecting the right Christmas gift didn't come easily.

As we perused the store, I meandered into the movie section, where I discovered an array of VHS tapes to choose from. For some reason, I was drawn to a collection of Bible stories. My gut told me they would enjoy this.

When I handed it to my dad, he asked me, "Would you want something like this?" I replied that I would. I remember the mixture of pride and disbelief on his face. What ten-year-old wants to watch a movie about the Bible?

For as long as I can remember, I have been drawn to depictions of the Bible on film. Whether it is a documentary about the hunt for Noah's ark or a dramatic presentation of the life of Jesus, I have longed to step into the world of the Bible, to find myself ever closer to the people and events that have shaped my life and guided my faith.

Sometimes the productions were great. What I'd imagined as I'd read the Bible felt as if it were coming to life on the screen. Other times, the quality wasn't nearly as good. The sets looked inaccurate.

The characters felt weak. It was as if the greatness of the Bible had been cheapened.

So it was with a hearty dose of skepticism that I watched *The Chosen* for the first time. The youth director at our church had been recommending it for months. The Facebook ads promoting it didn't seem to go away. So, when I sat down for lunch one day, I turned on the first episode.

That lunch break changed my life.

Something was different about this show. I was drawn into the lives of authentic Jews living in the first century. These weren't Christianized versions of Jewish believers, and this wasn't a stereotypical depiction of the first-century world. These writers had done their homework!

As I watched, I saw what it was like to be a Jew living in Israel at the time of Jesus. Details like how they taught the Scriptures to their children, the oppression they experienced from the Romans, the specific prayers they prayed throughout the day—things I had never seen before on-screen—were woven naturally into the show. Some of these were things that most people would probably miss, but they were included anyway because they mattered. They brought the world of Jesus to life.

At that moment, I felt compelled to do two things.

First, I knew I had to tell everyone I could about this show. It was something special, and people needed to know about it.

Second, I had to help people see the accurate things I saw, those contextual details embedded within the show that not only enriched each episode but also had the potential to transform how we read the Bible.

For instance, why did people fiercely hate tax collectors like Matthew? What was Simon sacrificing as he jumped out of his boat to follow Jesus? Why was the prayer Jesus recited with the children so essential to their faith? And how might the answers to those questions forever change the way we see these people, these passages, and even Scripture as a whole?

Soon after watching the first episode, I created a video highlighting details like these. I had been publishing YouTube videos for almost two years with little success, and I thought that perhaps this video might interest people and boost my channel.

> As I watched, I saw what it was like to be a Jew living in Israel at the time of Jesus. Details like how they taught the Scriptures to their children, the oppression they experienced from the Romans, the specific prayers they prayed throughout the day—things I had never seen before on-screen—were woven naturally into the show.

It didn't.

Well, at least, not at first. For about a month, nothing happened with the video. During that span, I actually "quit" YouTube. I was exhausted after working so hard for so long with nothing to show for it. So, I decided to take an extended break until I sensed God calling me back to this ministry.

A week later, God called me back to it.

Something happened to the video I had created about episode 1. Its views exploded! Within a matter of weeks, it went from one hundred views to one hundred *thousand* views. My channel went from eight hundred subscribers to eight thousand.

What I realized was that there is a hunger for insights like those in my video. People loved the show, but they also loved how it allowed them to immerse themselves in the world of Jesus and see the Bible in an entirely new way.

I may never know what changed to make the difference here. My best guess is that the algorithm figured out my niche, and I doubled down on that niche. It recognized content that this group liked (at first, just *The Chosen* content) and promoted it to them. The more I created, the more people it promoted it to, and things snowballed from there.

This book is written to help you do just that. I have broken it down by episode, with four chapters per episode. In each chapter, I highlight a specific moment or storyline in the episode, pointing out cultural and scriptural details that will both enhance your appreciation for the episode and expand your understanding of the Bible.

The Forgotten Teachings of Jesus: Rediscovering the Bible with The Chosen: *Season One* is about more than just learning interesting information and increasing your enjoyment of a television show, though. What I hope to show you through this first season is what it was like to be a disciple of Jesus. This is really at the heart of *The Chosen*, especially season 1. We get a unique glimpse into the life of a disciple, the sacrifices and commitments that were required, and how all of this is quite different from our modern understanding of "discipleship."

So, throughout the book, I am going to ask you questions and propose applications. I encourage you to take your time with them. Allow the Spirit to work through them. My hope is that the things you learn in this book will cause you to crave Scripture, to read God's

Word with new eyes, and to better understand the life of discipleship to which Jesus is calling each and every one of us.

The Chosen is an amazing series. But it is only amazing because of the story it tells: the greatest story ever told, the story of God's love for all of us, and the hope that we have in Jesus. May you experience these beautiful truths as you read this book. And may this be only the beginning of your journey deeper into God's Word.

Episode 1

TROUBLE

There is going to be trouble.

A woman is troubled by the demons that possess her.

The Romans are troubled by the revolutionary sentiment brewing within the Jewish community.

Two brothers are troubled by the oppressive taxes that threaten to take away their livelihood.

A tax collector is troubled by the hatred he faces from both Jews and Romans.

And yet, trouble is not necessarily a bad thing. By the end of episode 1, we will be introduced to a man who will stir up his own trouble. Ultimately, he will look upon all these characters and proclaim the powerful message we hear in the opening song:

> Oh, child, come on in
> Jump in the water
> Got no trouble with the mess you been
> [Come] Walk on the water

Chapter 1

HOPE IN TIMES OF TROUBLE

The night is cool along the Sea of Galilee. The scent of fish lingers in the air, drifting over from the port where merchants are closing up shop and fishermen are casting off to seek tomorrow's catch.

Close by, perhaps just across the field from Mount Arbel, a father sits with his daughter outside the tent that is their home. The girl awakens abruptly from a nightmare and comes to her father for comfort. He does what any first-century Jewish father would do in such a moment—he offers her the words of God's promise: "But now, thus says the LORD, who created you, O Jacob, and He who formed you, O Israel: 'Fear not, for I have redeemed you; I have called you by your name; you are Mine" (Isa. 43:1 NKJV).

Her father recites these words from memory. The words feel so natural, as if they are his common tongue, his *lingua franca*. He doesn't pause. He doesn't search. The words simply flow.

Through this touching moment, *The Chosen* gives us a bold introduction to the world of Jesus.

Unlike today, the people of Jesus' day didn't have personal copies of Scripture. Few if any had access to all the Hebrew Scriptures (the Old Testament). Even the local synagogue would have had only a handful of scrolls.

So, instead, the Jewish people would memorize Scripture. They would begin to learn it at an early age from whatever source they could, and they would recite it frequently throughout each day. In this tender exchange between father and daughter, the father is demonstrating this practice. He is helping his daughter to have God's Word written upon her heart, readily accessible wherever she is and in whatever she is going through.

But by opening the series with this particular verse from Isaiah, *The Chosen* is communicating something more. Obviously, these words would be comforting in and of themselves, a reminder that God will never abandon this little girl—that the Lord will see her through whatever is causing her to worry. But these words aren't meant just for her. This little girl is part of something much bigger than herself. And so are these words.

In fact, the comforting words spoken by Isaiah were written long before this girl was born, to a people living in a land far away from where she and her

> There were several factors that led to the paucity of Torah scrolls in local synagogues. One was space. When we look at the archaeology of first-century synagogues, their Torah closets were not large enough to hold all the books of the Torah. In Qumran, where portions of all but one of the Old Testament books were found, the scrolls take up cave after cave. Additionally, paper was expensive, and few men were equipped to copy these Scriptures. So, it is safe to assume that few, if any, towns had more than a handful of scrolls.

father resided. Isaiah wrote these words at a time when the Israelites had been removed from their land by the Babylonians. They were captives in a foreign country, and they had no idea when or if they would ever return home.

Nevertheless, Isaiah was promising that this was not the end of their story. He was telling them not to fear, for the Lord would redeem them, return them to their land, and set them free again. And, ultimately, that is precisely what the Lord did.

Unfortunately, it's possible to be liberated yet not truly free.

As the fictional father and daughter ponder these words at the beginning of the first century, their people are still longing for freedom. While the Jewish people had been back in their land for several centuries, they were still oppressed. Once again, they were captives, but this time it was in their own land. Rome had made them subjects of the Roman Empire. They had to submit to Roman rule but received none of the privileges that would have come had they been Roman citizens.

So, to them, the words of Isaiah were not merely a promise to those long past but also a prophecy for the future. They were crying out to be free, and they trusted that God was going to send a Savior, a Messiah, who would not merely remove Roman occupation but would also restore them to the glory and power of their forebears.

> The Pharisees "believed the Messiah would only arrive when Israel lived according to God's law." — Lois Tverberg and Ann Spangler

There was another source of trouble and concern, though. It was widely believed that one important change must happen before this Messiah would arise: The people must know and obey God's commands. Completely.[1]

When the Jewish religious leaders, like the Pharisees, looked at the oppression brought by the Roman Empire, they wondered why God was not rescuing Israel. Eventually, they concluded that the problem was that the Messiah couldn't come because the Jewish people were not properly obeying God's laws.

Torah can be a reference to both the first five books of the Old Testament and the entirety of the Hebrew Scriptures.

Consequently, at the time of Jesus, there was intense pressure for people to both know and obey the Torah. This makes the father's response to his daughter's fears all the more important. Not only is he offering her comfort by teaching her Scripture, but also he is teaching her Scripture by obeying Scripture.

In Deuteronomy 6, God commands his people, "Listen, O Israel! The LORD is our God, the LORD alone. And you must love the LORD your God with all your heart, all your soul, and all your strength. And you must commit yourselves wholeheartedly to these commands that I am giving you today. Repeat them again and again to your children" (vv. 4–7a NLT). These words come from a passage of Scripture called the *Shema* (pronounced shem-AW). It is one of the most important passages of Scripture in the Jewish community, a reminder of who God is and who God's people are to be. Faithful Jews recite it twice each day.

It has this name because *shema* is its opening word. It means "hear," but it also means "obey."

God was telling the Israelite people that they must know the law, obey the law, and pass the law down to their children. This was essential if the people were to remain faithful. And at the time of Jesus, they believed that it was essential in order for the Messiah to come.

The Jewish people would teach the Scripture while in their local synagogues, while doing work at home, when around the fire at night, and at every other opportunity. Just as we speak in our native tongue with little thought, Scripture became their common language, floating in and out of conversation naturally, often without need for explanation.

What's more, the community conversed not just in a handful of verses and stories; they discussed all of Scripture. They wrestled together with difficult and confusing passages. Children were taught not only "age-appropriate" stories, but even the stories that may scandalize many of us today.[2] Their mission was to pass down all of God's Word, and they didn't shy away from that responsibility.

They could do this because they did it as a community. They did it together. Good Jewish parents saw it as their responsibility to teach their own children the Torah, and the entire community saw this as a shared responsibility. They would draw upon the wisdom and insight of one another. And when difficult passages came up, they were prepared to explain them together.

From what we know of the Jewish education system, boys in Bet Sefer would memorize the first five books of the Bible. Additionally, Jewish people followed something called the *parasha*, which was basically lectionary that took them through the entire Torah over three years and through the first five books every year. So, children would have heard and discussed these Scriptures in synagogue from a very young age.

Insights like this make me keenly aware of how different things are today. Not only do many of us feel intimidated because we don't know enough about Scripture to explain it to our children, but also we feel alone in the task. When it comes to passing our faith on to our children, many of us tend to rely on the children's programs in our churches or Christian schools. But in each of these instances, we are disconnected from the process.

There are few places where we gather as a community to teach our children. So, while we may not share the same reasons for memorizing and passing down Scripture that the Jewish people did at the time of Jesus, we would do well to follow their example.

In the years to come, the little girl from this scene and the people of her community will learn that the Messiah will come whether or not they have mastered complete obedience to the law. But that does not negate the importance of knowing it.

To the people of Jesus' day, Scripture was a gift. Sometimes, they would even dance when it was read![3] And Scripture is still a gift.

As this first episode continues, we will discover that it is not only this young girl who finds herself in trouble. Every person we meet is in distress. All of their lives are dark and filled with conflict. In most cases, it is the absence of God's Word in their lives and a separation from the community that has led them to such a painful place.

But as we will soon see, God's Word is about to come into their lives to set them free.

Chapter 2

RABBIS AND ROMANS

The journey from Jerusalem to Galilee wasn't an easy one in the first century. Travelers were faced with a choice between two options. They could take the shorter route, which would lead them through Samaria. There they would be in a hostile land, susceptible to thieves who preyed upon anyone on the roads in this region. Alternatively, they could travel around Samaria. This would prolong their trip but ensure better protection. Avoiding Samaria would also let them make a statement about what Jews thought of Samaritans. More on that later.

Either way, the journey would not be a short one. It would take days, perhaps even a week. Travelers would journey down from Jerusalem along mountainous paths and be exposed to the blazing sun or torrential rains that led to sudden floods. But when they finally arrived at their destination, they would find themselves in a fertile region surrounding a beautiful lake.

The Sea of Galilee was central to life in Israel at the time of Jesus. It was teeming with fish. Its waters supplied the Jordan River. Around it curved some of the most important roads and trade routes in Israel.

Despite its importance, the region of Galilee was viewed as provincial and uncultured compared to Jerusalem. And worse, it was a hotbed of revolutionary activity.

In this episode, we meet Nicodemus, a Jewish leader and teacher. Someone of Nicodemus's stature, a Pharisee of high pedigree, may not have relished being sent to an area like Galilee. Neither would Quintus, the Roman he encounters toward the end of his journey from Jerusalem to Capernaum.

The character Quintus is portrayed as the praetor of Galilee, a representative of the Roman Empire, which holds authority over Nicodemus, the young girl and her father, and all the Jews in Israel. He is a soldier and a politician, responsible for maintaining peace and order in the region. Rome valued order and despised rebellion. Its mission was to spread the Roman way of life throughout the world to demonstrate that all lives would be better under Roman rule.

A stone dating to AD 9 was discovered at Priene, an ancient Greek city in western Turkey, bearing an inscription that described the birth of Emperor Augustus as *euangelion*—the same word the angel of the Lord uses when pronouncing the birth of Jesus to the shepherds in Luke 2. Euangelion is a declaration of "good news," a proclamation that people's lives will be better because of a certain event or circumstance. Rome used this word when referring to the influence of the emperor and his empire. Christians used it to refer to Jesus and his coming kingdom.

But Quintus has a problem, one he believes Nicodemus should share: Messianic fervor is growing in Galilee. Revolutionary whispers are spreading. This is seen in the episode when a sick man asks a passing tax collector if he is the Messiah and when we see graffiti on a building proclaiming that the Messiah will destroy the Romans. Quintus needs to maintain order, and he expects Nicodemus to help him.

Nicodemus is described as the "teacher of teachers." Rather than being a formal title, this is a generic proclamation that he is a "rabbi of rabbis," a teacher of the ones responsible for teaching the rest of Israel. In other words, Nicodemus is a prominent religious leader. Quintus knows that people will listen to him, so he reminds Nicodemus that it is in his own best interest to quiet these revolutionary undertones. If he doesn't, his people will suffer.

What we see here is the meeting of two men who perhaps have the most to lose with the possible arrival of a violent, revolutionary Messiah.

Rome has seen what messianic fervor can do. Just decades earlier, uprisings in Galilee had led to a violent revolution in Sepphoris, a town just three miles from Nazareth. Sepphoris was ultimately destroyed, and thousands of Jews were carted away into slavery.[1] Rome would not hesitate to do so again if the situation repeated itself.

If Quintus allows rebellion to erupt in Galilee, he will be shamed. He will likely be relieved of his post, and his future prospects will be extinguished. So, as this revolutionary fervor grows, he must take swift and harsh action, preventing such rebellion before it breaks out.

Yet, while Quintus might appear to casually command Nicodemus to resolve this situation in their exchange along the road, the task before Nicodemus is not a simple one.

Today, we tend to view the Jews of the Bible as one homogenous group. We assume they all believed the same things and practiced their religion in exactly the same way. We lump various Jewish groups into the category of "enemies of Jesus," supposing that they were unified in both their theology and their attitude toward Jesus.

This was certainly not the case.

Just as Christians are diverse today, so were Jews at the time of Jesus. There were sects and subsects. Their leaders divided into different camps.

> Zealots saw it as their God-ordained responsibility to violently oppose Rome, and they believed that the Messiah would come to exercise political and military might. They were just waiting for a Messiah to lead them.

If Nicodemus is to fulfill Quintus's demands, he must navigate all of this. Not only must he determine the various sources of rebellion, but also he must consider their unique beliefs, their relationships with one another, and the specific solutions that will appease each of them.

For instance, one of the strongest opponents of Rome in Galilee was a group called the Zealots. They rightly considered Rome to be foreign invaders, pagans who were oppressing their people and threatening their way of life. From their perspective, violence was the only solution. Just as their ancestors had risen up and defeated the Seleucids in the Maccabean war nearly two hundred years earlier, so they believed they were destined to overthrow Rome.[2] In fact, they believed that the Messiah would be sent to help them do this.[3]

Another sect of Jews in Israel at the time was the Essenes. The Essenes also believed that Rome did not belong in Israel. They too had witnessed the corruption and oppression of their people. But unlike the Zealots, rather than resorting to violence, they decided to move to remote regions and form strict communities that would closely follow the Torah. This group produced the documents we know as the Dead Sea Scrolls.

These sects, however, did not blame Rome alone for the downfall of their nation; they also blamed the Jewish religious leaders. They believed that these men submitted to Rome too frequently, allowing the Torah to be compromised so they might achieve their own goals. For example, the Zealots would sometimes even assassinate Jewish leaders whom they believed to be especially corrupt.

Quintus is placing Nicodemus in the middle of all of this. He forces upon him a problem that has no easy solutions. How can Nicodemus convince diverse groups like the Zealots and Essenes to agree on a nonviolent solution? How can he gain their trust when he, as a Pharisee and member of the Sanhedrin, is part of the Jewish leadership they condemn?

What we glimpse in just the first few minutes of *The Chosen* is the tension swirling throughout the region at this time. There is a spirit of discontent, a lack of unity. Quintus and Nicodemus couldn't know it yet, but more strife is just on the horizon. The Jewish people are already at odds over their faith, and they will be at odds over the Messiah. They will question if they should trust him. They will debate whether or not he meets their expectations or the prophecies of Scripture. Rome will deem him a threat to their mission, an opponent to their emperor, and a challenger to their very core beliefs.

One specific example of this is when the high priest Ananias was assassinated by Zealots. "He was a typical Sadducee, wealthy, haughty, unscrupulous, filling his sacred office for purely selfish and political ends, antinationalist in his relation to the Jews, friendly to the Romans. He died an ignominious death, being assassinated by the popular zealots (sicarii) at the beginning of the last Jewish war."[4]

In the end, the Romans and Jews would join forces to crucify Jesus. This has confused people for millennia. How did the Jewish leaders convince the Romans to agree to execute Jesus by means of the worst form of capital punishment available at that time? How did they both come to decide that Jesus had to die? This scene on the road between Quintus and Nicodemus highlights some of those answers.

> Some Jewish sects strongly opposed one another because of their, in some cases, wildly diverse theological beliefs. For instance, Sadducees only accepted the first five books of the Bible and denied resurrection. This was far different from the beliefs of the Pharisees and Essenes.

Even before Jesus' ministry began, the foundations for an alliance between rabbis and Romans had been laid. If the Messiah came and was disruptive, he wouldn't alleviate the tension in Israel; he would elevate it. To Romans and the Jewish religious leaders, the status quo might not be ideal, but it was better than the alternative. The Romans wanted to maintain their empire, and the Jewish religious leaders wanted to maintain their positions in society. A revolutionary Messiah would bring nothing but chaos, and neither group could allow that to happen.

Yet, while the Messiah would cause strife for some, he would unite others. Jesus sparked a movement not only of opposition but also of those who wanted to be part of the kingdom he was building.

Chapter 3

THE MOST HATED MAN IN CAPERNAUM

Somewhere in Rome, a tradesman gathered his goods to sell. He passed them along to a caravan that would travel thousands of miles through Roman provinces, across mountains, along seas, and down into what was then called Judea.

The tradesman knew that there was demand for his wares in this region. Roman men and women were living far away from home, confined to a region with little culture and even fewer traditional comforts. Praetors, soldiers, and politicians longed for items that would display their importance and give them an edge over their peers. There was money to be made. So, the tradesman endured the risks to offer his goods for sale.

After the long journey, these goods eventually found their way down the Via Maris trade route to the city of Capernaum. The Hebrew name for this town is *Kfar Nahum* (pronounced *k'far na-oom*), the "village of comfort." For these weary travelers, it certainly lived up to its name. Capernaum was an important destination after a long journey.

But Capernaum would become important for other reasons. It was here where Jesus would base his ministry. It was here where two brothers named Simon and Andrew would run their fishing business. And it is here where the filmmakers imagine that a troubled man named Matthew will collect taxes from the Jewish people.

We meet Matthew in episode 1, and we immediately notice two things: he is wealthy, and he is afraid. Everything about Matthew's home shows that he lives in opulence. He has rows of expensive shoes, so many that he can dispose of a pair without any concern for cost. His clothes are expensive. His haircut is Roman. Everything about him seems designed to elicit cringes, jealousy, and animosity from his fellow Jews.

Saying that Matthew was the most hated man in Capernaum is my way of commenting about tax collectors and their place in society. While there may have actually been a more hated man in Capernaum at the time, I'm pointing out a place where the show is depicting the context correctly.

We also see that this wealth has come at a high cost. Matthew is afraid. We learn that Matthew has hired a driver to transport him into town. But his goal is not to arrive in a carriage, entering with pomp and power. Instead, Matthew hides under a sheet, afraid to even be seen by the people along his journey. He is the most hated man in Capernaum, and he knows it.

The truth is, while Jews despised the Romans, they would have detested Matthew even more. Romans were foreign invaders, but Matthew was one of their own, a Jew who had betrayed his people.

As in every generation, the people of Jesus' day did not relish paying taxes. But to make matters worse, they weren't paying taxes to their own government. This was not a system within which they could nominate representatives and influence laws. No, they were being taxed by Rome, their oppressors.

Rome imposed a variety of taxes. There were the *tributum soli* (land tax) and the *tributum capitis* (head tax), for example, taxes whose amounts were determined by the most recent census of that region. There were also taxes on goods and transactions. What made these taxes so unbearable was that they not only took funds from an already impoverished people but also provided very little benefit to them. Most Jews were not Roman citizens, which meant they were paying for services and benefits they did not receive. This was likely a significant source of the revolutionary tension in the region.

Scripture points out that Paul is a Roman citizen (Acts 22:28). It highlights this because it was not normal for a Jew. This gave him benefits and access that most Jews did not enjoy.

What made matters worse was how these taxes were collected. Rather than collecting the money itself, Rome would outsource this responsibility to locals. These Jewish men would purchase the privilege of collecting taxes— and a privilege it was!

If a man was selected to be a tax collector, he would pay Rome in advance for the taxes he was expecting to collect in that region.[1] Then he would go out and collect not only what was owed by each person but also an amount on top of that as a commission for himself. Beyond that, tax collectors would frequently stop traders along the highway, demanding a portion of their money or goods.

This, of course, led to widespread greed and corruption among tax collectors. They became very wealthy, while the people around them became more and more impoverished. Worse yet, they were bankrupting their own people in the name of Rome, aiding the oppressor and profiting from it.

Because of tax collectors' corruption, the rabbis (local Jewish religious leaders) declared them to be ritually unclean. This meant that they were cut off from Jewish society, culture, and worship. Their fellow Jews were not allowed to associate with them. This is why Matthew is so cautious in the early scenes of this episode. It's also why Rome assigns him an armed guard. These soldiers are primarily protecting the tax revenue that is being collected, but they're also protecting Matthew.

So, while Matthew may have been one of the wealthiest men in Capernaum, he was also probably one of the loneliest. Not only would the Jewish community have avoided contact with him, but it's possible that his own family would have disowned him. In order to retain good standing in Jewish society, they would have likely cut off ties with the one seen to be in the wrong.

In Matthew, we find someone who is in a different kind of trouble. Though he is valuable to Rome and extremely successful, he is alone.

When the Messiah comes, he will be a threat to Matthew's livelihood and position, just as he is for Nicodemus and Quintus. But he will offer Matthew something that all his money and influence cannot buy: community.

When Jesus later calls Matthew to be his disciple, he is intentionally setting himself in opposition to the Jewish religious leaders. People will wonder how anyone can listen to a rabbi who consorts with a tax collector. They will ask each other what kind of rabbi would associate so closely with a man whom other religious leaders have deemed unclean.

There is a cost to choosing imperfect people such as us to be Jesus' disciples. There are challenges that come with putting the work of the kingdom in the hands of those who are far too often sinful and selfish.

For Jesus, the price of choosing disciples like us was his life.

Chapter 4

A DIFFERENT KIND OF TROUBLE

As the character named Lilith gazes upon the heavens, she sees a sky not altogether different from the one of her childhood. We come to understand that she was that little girl who had recited the Scripture with her father as the episode began. Back then, she lived in Magdala, a town just a few miles down the coast of the Sea of Galilee from Capernaum.[1]

Like Capernaum, Magdala was a fishing village. But rather than catching fish, the people of Magdala primarily processed fish, preserving and selling them along the Via Maris, the road that ran along the western side of the Sea of Galilee and down through Israel.[2]

> "Pickling of fish was much praised along the shores of the Sea of Galilee, which has excellent fish (Magdala). Much pickling was also done along the shores of the Mediterranean and in the Gulf of Elath. This may well explain the presence of the quantities of fish bones found among kitchen refuse on many sites in the Negev and in Transjordan."
> — Avraham Negev

As she looks up at that same sky and out over the sea, Lilith is reminded of the words her father taught her that night so long ago: "But now, thus says the LORD, who created you, O Jacob, and He who formed you, O Israel: 'Fear not, for I have redeemed you; I have called you by your name; you are Mine'" (Isa. 43:1 NKJV).

Though these words are still written upon her heart, they feel empty. Has God actually redeemed her? Her circumstances say otherwise.

Lilith (whose name, we later learn, is actually Mary) now lives in the Red Quarter, a neighborhood of ill repute in Capernaum. In episode 1, the level of Lilith's participation in immoral activities is somewhat unknown. But what becomes very clear is that Lilith is demon-possessed.

"Red Quarter" is not a biblical term, nor is there evidence Capernaum had such a part of town. However, it reflects very real circumstances of the time. Gambling, prostitution, and other illicit businesses were considered unacceptable, if not explicitly forbidden, within the Jewish community. Nevertheless, they were unavoidable, and to a certain degree, tolerated.

Luke's gospel testifies to this, saying that there were among Jesus' followers "some women who had been healed of evil spirits and diseases: [including] Mary (who was called Magdalene), from whom seven demons had gone out" (8:2).

Luke was telling us that Mary was very sick. She was possessed by not one but seven demons. Now, perhaps that means she had seven distinct demons possessing her at once or that she had undergone several previous exorcisms and was now possessed by a seventh demon. In Hebrew culture, the number seven is also the number for completion. So, this could be Luke's way of telling us that Lilith wasn't just possessed; she was *completely* possessed. It consumed her whole life, and she was a prisoner of her affliction.

The Bible doesn't record how or when Mary was delivered from this possession, but it's reasonable to speculate that Jesus had done this for her at some point. *The Chosen* suggests that Lilith's condition has relegated her to the lowest circles of society. Such societal rejection may surprise or even upset us today. Why should someone be punished for something that was not her fault? Who would ever choose to be possessed by a demon? But in first-century Jewish culture, people saw Lilith's situation differently.

At that time, people considered things like sickness and possession to be consequences of sin. To be stricken in this way was thought to be God's punishment either for a sin one had committed or even for a sin an ancestor had committed (see Job 4:7–9; Luke 13:1–5; and John 9:1–2, for example). This superstition extended to both physical and spiritual ailments.

As a result, people did not want to be associated with the diseased or the possessed. To associate with the person was to associate with his or her sin. And such sin brought shame and could result in the person being cast out from the society until cleansing could be performed.

So, as with Matthew, Lilith's life is very lonely. The only people who appear to accept her are those who have themselves been rejected.

But possession isn't the only reason Lilith is marked with shame. In this episode, we see a flashback to when Lilith was assaulted by a Roman soldier. *The Chosen* omits the graphic details, but it is obvious that Lilith still carries the effects of this violent act.

Unfortunately, this too may have led to Lilith's low standing in the community. Jewish law was clear about sexual assault, and it prescribed various responses to such situations. For example:

> If a man happens to meet in a town a virgin pledged
> to be married and he sleeps with her, you shall take

both of them to the gate of that town and stone
them to death—the young woman because she was
in a town and did not scream for help, and the man
because he violated another man's wife. You must
purge the evil from among you....

If a man happens to meet a virgin who is not pledged
to be married and rapes her and they are discovered,
he shall pay her father fifty shekels of silver. He must
marry the young woman, for he has violated her.
He can never divorce her as long as he lives. (Deut.
22:23–24, 28–29 NIV)

In episode 1, Lilith finds herself caught between these two laws.
She was within the town limits when the attack occurred. But since
she was being attacked by a Roman soldier, not only would her screams
have gone unanswered; they would likely have brought her further
harm from the soldier. Furthermore, there is no chance that this soldier will marry her, which means that she will be left with this shame,
deemed unmarriageable by her community.

Ultimately, Lilith is first shamed by the assault, then shamed
again in the eyes of the community. If people believe that she hadn't
screamed, they will judge her as guilty under the law. They may even
assume that her demon possession is a consequence of this supposedly
voluntary behavior.

To make matters worse, Lilith has no one to defend her. Her father
has died. She apparently has no brothers. In this patriarchal society,
she is virtually helpless.

Lilith is in trouble.

But in her moment of deepest pain, standing at the edge of a cliff, one step away from ending her life, Lilith finds hope in the form of a white dove that leads her back to her neighborhood tavern, the Hammer. As she sits at the bar, hoping to numb the pain within her, Jesus approaches. But rather than welcoming Jesus, her immediate response is to flee.

How often in our lives are we tempted to flee from God's grace, perhaps because we're not ready for it or are fearful that we are not worthy of it?

Similar to his relationship with Matthew (or any of us), Jesus seemingly has nothing to gain from befriending Lilith. In this honor/shame culture, simply associating with her is enough to tarnish his name. But rather than fearing the trouble she will cause him, he frees her from the trouble she has been enduring for far too long.

Jesus pursues Lilith as she runs from the bar. The way he sparks her transformation is especially important.

He says her name.

She may have been instantly reminded of her father quoting Isaiah's reminder that the Lord had called Israel *by name*.

In Hebrew culture, a name was more than a word assigned to you at birth; a name was your identity. To bear someone's name meant that you represented that person. You carried his or her power and authority. You deserved the same honor and respect.

In her shame, she had abandoned her true name, surrendering to the lesser life of a made-up person called Lilith. So, to set her free, Jesus calls her by her real name: Mary. And with that one word, everything changes.

Mary realizes that Jesus sees her not for who she has become but for who she truly is. She is more than her mistakes, more than her circumstances. She is a child of God. And now she is free.

Too often, it is easy for us to get lost in our shame, surrendering ourselves to the lies that tell us we are less than who God created us to be. Every day, we are surrounded by people who feel just like Mary did: rejected for their sins, prisoners to a past that determines their present and predicts their future, suffering from a pain that no one seems to understand.

Perhaps you feel this way sometimes. You know all too well the pain of Lilith, or of Matthew, or even of the Israelite people as a whole. You have faced the troubles of this world. You have been marred by your mistakes and shunned for your decisions, and you have struggled with your faith.

> Mary realizes that Jesus sees her not for who she has become but for who she truly is. She is more than her mistakes, more than her circumstances. She is a child of God. And now she is free.

This episode of *The Chosen* highlights something we read in Scripture and can now see played out on the screen: none of these things keeps us from Jesus.

Jesus didn't come to call those who are worthy, because no one deserves salvation. He doesn't require perfection. Jesus came to proclaim the good news that the Messiah has come and the world will be different. The standards and expectations of the past are about to change. The humble will be exalted, and the exalted will be humbled.

The Word of God has been made flesh, and people are about to see the heart of God revealed in their midst.

For some, this will be the long-awaited liberation from their troubles. But as we will see in the next episode, for others, their troubles are just about to begin.

Episode 2

REST

As the sun sets and light begins to fade over the Sea of Galilee, families are hastily closing up shops, securing animals, and making final preparations for *Shabbat* (pronounced *sha-bawt*). For the next twenty-four hours, the day of the Sabbath, life will proceed at a much different pace. People will rest. This is how God said it should be.

But rest comes in many different forms.

For some, rest means a brief nap and a break from work. For others, rest is a few minutes alone, free from the distractions and responsibilities of daily life.

Then there are those for whom rest is needed in a much deeper sense. There is a stirring in their souls that just won't go away. Whether it derives from the harshness of their circumstances or a nagging dilemma that will not subside, they long to be at peace, to rest from the burdens that overwhelm them.

In episode 2, we witness how an entire community structures their lives in hopes of rest. In the end, we will be reintroduced to the One who shows them both what true rest really looks like and where to find it, the One who promises, "Come to me, all of you who labor and are burdened, and I will give you rest" (Matt. 11:28).

Chapter 5

HISTORY AND MEMORY

The Sea of Galilee has been called by several names throughout history: Lake Kinneret, the Lake of Gennesaret, the Sea of Tiberias; and in the Old Testament, it is referred to by still another name: *Yam-kinnereth*, or the Sea of Chinnereth. This is the name *The Chosen* displays as episode 2 begins.

In the prologue, a family is gathering near Chinnereth sometime during the reign of King Solomon. As members of this family scurry around the camp, a young boy named Eli points to the sky and declares that he sees a star. He is hoping that this marks the official beginning of Shabbat.

Shabbat is the Hebrew word for "rest." But its meaning runs deeper than that. It also represents the day that God commanded God's people to rest.

The word *kinnereth* appears in passages such as Numbers 34:11, Deuteronomy 3:17, Joshua 13:27, and others. In many Bibles, however, this word is translated "Galilee" for the sake of the reader.

In the fourth commandment, God commands the Hebrew people:

> Remember the day of the Sabbath, to consecrate
> it. Six days you will work, and you will do all your
> work. But the seventh day is a Sabbath for Yahweh
> your God; you will not do any work—you or your
> son or your daughter, your male slave or your female
> slave, or your animal, or your alien who is in your
> gates—because in six days Yahweh made the heavens
> and the earth, the sea and all that is in them, and on
> the seventh day he rested. Therefore Yahweh blessed
> the seventh day and consecrated it. (Ex. 20:8–11)

Shabbat is central to Jewish life. The entire week revolves around
it. To understand why, it is important to consider what was happening
when God gave this command to the Hebrew people.

As Moses stood on Mount Sinai, receiving the Ten
Commandments from God, the Hebrew people were still getting used
to the taste of freedom. For hundreds of years, they had been slaves in
Egypt. Their parents had been slaves, as had their grandparents and
great-grandparents. No person in their community had ever known
freedom. The Hebrews were born slaves, taught to be slaves, and were
expected to bring forth a future generation of slaves.

So, when God brought the Hebrew people out of Egypt, one of the
first things he did was teach them how *not* to be slaves.

Each of the Ten Commandments outlines both what it looks like
to be a free people and how to maintain this freedom. God's people,
the Israelites, must worship the Lord and no other gods. They must
honor their parents and one another. And they must learn how to rest.

Shabbat is critical to this. During their centuries of slavery, the Hebrew people had worked day in and day out without rest. They worked out of fear, surrendered to someone else's control.

But now they were free! And free people rest.

This doesn't come naturally, though, to people who have never known anything but slavery. Through the fourth commandment and subsequent passages in the Torah, God teaches the Israelite people both the importance of rest and how to experience it. God helps them see that rest is an opportunity to trust in the Lord and to believe that the same God who freed them from slavery will always provide for them—even when they rest.

God simply wants time to be with them and to have a recurring opportunity to deepen and strengthen the relationship between him and his people. Because the stronger their relationship is with the Lord, the less likely they are to fall back into slavery.

This is why Shabbat has been such a central part of Jewish life for thousands of years. Over the centuries, many traditions have arisen surrounding the celebration of Shabbat. Several of these are illustrated in this opening scene.

For instance, soon after young Eli points out the star, a man says, "A woman of valor, who can find? Far beyond jewels is her value." This is part of a song called the "Eshet Chayil" (pronounced *ey-shet chah-yeel*). Later, a woman looks to Eli and says, "May God make you like Ephraim and Manasseh." A man then looks to a young girl and says, "May God make you like Sarah, Rebekah, Rachel, and Leah." These are traditional blessings spoken over children at the beginning of Shabbat.

All of these statements are drawn directly from Scripture. The "Eshet Chayil" comes from Proverbs 31. The declaration "May God make you like Ephraim and Manasseh" comes from Genesis 48:20.

In the Jewish community, Scripture wasn't just something to be read in the synagogue. It was more than a list of dos and don'ts or ancient words recorded by some strange people.

Scripture was their memory.

These were the tales of the Israelites' ancestors, their family. They believed they were words that God was still speaking to the current generation. By recalling these Scriptures each week, they were teaching their children their identity. They were reminding them that they had once been slaves, but now they were free. And they were instilling in them the relationship with God that would keep them free.

> Rest is an opportunity to trust in the Lord and to believe that the same God who freed them from slavery will always provide for them—even when they rest.

For the people in this opening scene, this is relatively easy. They are living during Solomon's reign, a time of prosperity.

But soon things would change. The twelve tribes of Israel would be divided. Weak and unfaithful kings would come to power. The people would be led away from the Lord. And eventually, the land would be overtaken by foreign invaders.

By the time of Jesus, though much had happened to shape the land and the nation, not much had changed in the hearts of the people. They were divided, their leaders were corrupt, and yet another foreign power controlled their land.

After centuries of this, the people were tired. This long struggle was exhausting. And in that atmosphere, God's people began not only to cry out in distress but also to cling to their faith by looking for the answer to their cries: a Messiah who would free them from all of this, a Savior who would finally give them rest.

How often do we find ourselves in a similar position? We let our relationship with the Lord slip. We follow weak leaders—or ourselves. We immerse ourselves in busyness and distractions.

Until one day it all catches up with us. We find ourselves lost and exhausted, overwhelmed and confused. The path we chose did not lead us to the destination we'd hoped. We find ourselves crying out to the Lord, asking God to free us from our burdens and give us rest from our weariness.

The more we read Scripture, the more we see that we are not all that different from those who came before us. We long for a Savior, and so did they.

But as we will see, the wait is over. The Messiah is here. However, things may not be as we expected.

Chapter 6

WHO IS YOUR DOMINUS?

History has a way of succumbing to the perspective of both its author and its audience. To a Roman in the first century, Galilee was a backwater territory, devoid of Roman culture and values, rife with conflict, but also essential to Rome's control of trade and transport. The people inhabiting this land were confusing. They worshipped only one god, were incredibly restrictive in their diet, and vehemently rejected both the Roman Empire and the values for which it stood.

A Jew living in Galilee at the same time would have had a much different perspective. He would have seen Rome as the oppressor, the foreign invader staking illegal claim to a land that

> History is presented and interpreted through the biases of those who tell it. As an audience, we too interpret and respond to history based on how we view the world. Even though Jesus was a Jewish rabbi who strictly observed the law, our bias might be that the law is bad, so we will imprint that upon Jesus, thus altering how we both interpret history and share it.

God had given to Israel. He would have considered Rome's customs immoral, their gods false, and their behavior brutal.

> The American Founders were fascinated by the Roman Republic and its key figures. The most famous play in the eighteenth century, beloved by George Washington especially, was *Cato*, which influenced the way people thought and the discourse of the time. Our government is based on many Roman ideals.

Who we are and the circumstances we face determine how we view both our own situation and the situations of others. The average eighteenth-century American might side with Rome, since so much of American culture at that time was built on Roman values. A nineteenth-century person in India, however, might empathize with the Jews, as they, too, knew what it was like to live under colonial rule.

As Christians today, our perspective on the first-century environment of the Gospels might seem obvious. We think that if we had lived in that culture at that time, of course we would have supported Jesus and his people against Rome!

But is it that simple?

In episode 2, we return to Matthew the tax collector. In one scene, he has been called in to speak to Quintus, the praetor of the region. As a military official, Quintus represents Rome and its authority. He expects Matthew to give to him the same respect and allegiance that each citizen owes to Rome itself.

For this reason, Matthew addresses Quintus in a very specific way. He calls him *dominus*.

On the surface, dominus might seem like little more than a respectful way to address someone in Quintus's position. But its meaning runs deeper than that. *Dominus* is the Latin word that means "master" or even "lord."

This was a term that communicated true subservience. Slaves used it to address their owners. And while Quintus might not own Matthew, Matthew's deference makes clear the nature of this relationship: Quintus has control over Matthew. He has the power to decide whether Matthew keeps his job or doesn't, whether he thrives or dies. If Matthew wants to rise in wealth and prosperity, he must surrender to, honor, and serve Quintus completely.

This relationship is but a small reflection of the relationship that all Roman subjects were expected to have with their emperor. Throughout the empire, people would greet one another and address the emperor with shouts of "Caesar is Lord." They were expected to make it clear to all who they worshipped and served.

For Jews (and eventually Christians), this posed a very grave choice. If they wanted to prosper and retain what level of freedom they had, they would have to declare their fealty to the emperor. But to do so to the extent the Romans expected would amount to worship, and that would compromise their relationship with God.

Scripture had long been clear that God's people were to serve no one but God alone. He is their Lord, their Master, their one true Dominus. Over time, Jewish people came to believe that the name of God was so holy that it should not even be spoken. Instead, they used the word *Adonai* to refer to God. *Adonai* (pronounced *add-o-nahy*) means "Lord" or "master," just like *dominus*.

This means that every Jew was faced with a difficult question: Who will be my dominus? Will it be Caesar or will it be God? Because to worship one, they must withhold devotion from the other.

There was another factor that made this situation difficult. Not long after the death of Julius Caesar, Augustus, the first Roman emperor, declared that whoever ruled as Caesar was actually a god. And since Augustus was the grandnephew and adopted son of Caesar, he was referred to throughout the empire as the "son of god."

So, for a Jew to worship the emperor, a man adorned with such a title, would be a direct violation of the first commandment. Israel was to have no other gods but the Lord. God made it clear that such false worship would not set them free (as Rome promised)—it would destroy them.

Matthew is well aware of all this as he stands before Quintus. He is Jewish. His family raised him to worship the Lord. He knows the importance of the title he uses to address Quintus.

But the episode suggests that Matthew's allegiance has strayed. He sees Rome offering something that God has never provided for his people, at least in recent history: rest.

Rather than fighting each day to oppose Rome, Matthew sees an opportunity to join it. While God has allowed the Jewish people to be conquered by one nation after another, Rome appears to have brought order to the world. They have conquered vast territories and implemented systems and structures that guide and control the empire. Perhaps for someone like Matthew, these would seem to be things that God had never delivered. In his eyes, both his future and the future of his people are brighter when allied with Rome.

Have you ever found yourself in a situation like that? Are we really that much different from Matthew?

It is easy to believe that we would naturally have stood with God's people rather than Rome. But aren't we often tempted as Matthew was? Aren't we surrounded by people and products that promise to make our lives better? That vie for our time, our money, our thoughts, and our passion, which all belong first to God? And aren't we sometimes tempted to give in?

Each day, we must wrestle with the same question that Matthew does: Who will be my dominus?

Will it be my job? My favorite leader? My inner temptations?

What will have my greatest allegiance?

Will it be the Lord? Or will it be something else?

Because, as Matthew will learn, unless it is the former, we will never truly find rest.

Chapter 7

THE THREAT OF A MIRACLE

One thing is certain about Jesus: He changes things. His very presence makes an indelible impact on the lives of those he encounters. Not all people receive this change positively, though. What might bring rest to some may end up causing chaos for others.

This is certainly the case for Nicodemus in episode 2. After failing in his attempt to exorcise the demons from Lilith (Mary Magdalene) in the first episode, Nicodemus now learns that she has been healed, though he knows it did not happen through him. There is only one problem now: people believe that Nicodemus performed the exorcism.

Nicodemus is summoned before a man called the *av bet din* (pronounced *av-bayt-deen*). The phrase *bet din* means "house of judgment," making the av bet din the "father" of the court. This man was the chief judge of the Sanhedrin, the ruling Jewish court at that time. In this episode, he has heard of a reported exorcism, and it is his task to determine whether or not this exorcism was real, and if Nicodemus acted correctly in his performance of it.[1]

For Nicodemus, though he already holds high position and stature, an exorcism would nevertheless be an incredible accomplishment. He is a member of the Sanhedrin, a Pharisee, a rabbi of rabbis. This would affirm God's anointing on his life.

> One thing is certain about Jesus: He changes things. His very presence makes an indelible impact on the lives of those he encounters.

But as we know from watching episode 1, it is not Nicodemus who heals Lilith. It's Jesus. When Nicodemus learns what actually happened, this creates an entirely new set of concerns. Who is this mysterious rabbi who can cast out demons? On whose authority is he acting?

The Pharisees adhered strictly to both the written law and the oral traditions. There were standards and procedures for things like exorcisms. The show depicts leaders who are responsible for granting such authority to others. But through this miracle, Jesus is disrupting that system. Some will believe that he undermines and threatens the very religious systems that undergird Jewish society.

Nicodemus isn't just worried about what this miracle worker is doing. He is worried about who this man might be. This miracle Lilith experienced was a work of God beyond human understanding. The man who performed it may very well be the Messiah for whom the people have been waiting, the one who will bring true salvation.

This possibility brings Nicodemus both rest and unrest. Rest because this may mean that the promised Messiah has arrived. But unrest too, because based on the stories Nicodemus has been hearing, this Messiah might not be who they expect. In fact, by allegedly driving out demons and doing other things that only God can do, he appears to be claiming to be more than who they are expecting.

To truly understand this concern, we have to look closely at something Mary (who no longer calls herself Lilith) says to Nicodemus when he interviews her. He presses her to explain how Jesus healed her. But all she knows to answer is, "I was one way ... and now I am completely different. And the thing that happened in between ... was him."

In and of itself, there is nothing concerning about this statement. It is what Mary says next that would frighten Nicodemus and his fellow religious leadership, a specific word that adds even more gravity to what Jesus has done. Mary says that Jesus told her that she is *redeemed*.

In Hebrew, this is the word *ga'al* (pronounced *ga-ahl*). It means to set someone free. Often, it is used in reference to God's liberation of the Hebrew people from Egyptian slavery (e.g., Ex. 6:6; 18:10). But those familiar with Jewish family systems would have recognized that Jesus' use of this word has even deeper implications.

In a Hebrew family unit, the father of the family, the *bet av*, was responsible for everyone in his household: spouses, children, servants, and so on. If someone in the family got in trouble, the bet av would be responsible for "redeeming" (*g'ulah*) that person. In a sense, this individual belonged to him and was his to reclaim.

So, by using this word to describe what he has done to Mary, Jesus declares that she belongs to him. He has come to redeem her as his own. But he isn't redeeming her from just any situation; he is redeeming her from sin, shame, and demonic possession. He is redeeming her, in other words, from those things that only God can redeem us from.

For Nicodemus, this poses an incredible challenge. Despite Quintus's warning about what would happen if a disruptive Messiah were to arise, Nicodemus believes he is ready to embrace the long-expected Messiah. But if this man, Jesus, is claiming to be something more than that, if he is in fact claiming to be God in the flesh, is this too much to believe? Is it blasphemy?

Nicodemus is wrestling with a dilemma that many Pharisees and religious leaders faced at the time of Jesus: Are this man's claims true? And if so, what does that do to those things we already believe and hold dear?

From Scripture, we know that Jesus eventually attracted several followers who were Pharisees, including Nicodemus (see Acts 15:5 and John 19:39). But we also see instances when Jesus ran afoul of such religious leaders. In their eyes, Jesus' teachings went too far, disrupted too much. In the end, most religious leaders rejected him to preserve the teachings and beliefs they held most dear.

Today, we are still faced with this dilemma when presented with the gospel. The gospel is certain to disrupt our lives. While it will bring us rest from our burdens, it will also create its own measure of unrest. If we are to follow Jesus, we must be transformed, and transformation by its very definition means change. Our devotion to Jesus may call into question our relationships, ambitions, systems, and comforts.

In the end, we will all be forced to choose: Will I, like Nicodemus, be drawn back to the life I've always known? Or like Mary, will I be able to look back and say, "I was one way, and now I am different. And the thing that happened in between was him"?

Chapter 8

VERY DIFFERENT DINNERS

After Alexander the Great began to build his empire in the fourth century BC, two significant events occurred that would impact the Israelite people hundreds of years later. First, Alexander imposed a new culture. Whenever Alexander would conquer an area, he would integrate his own Greek culture into the regions he conquered. He would have his soldiers intermarry with the people they had conquered. He introduced the Greek language, philosophy, and customs. This campaign was called *Hellenization*.

Second, Alexander's empire became so large that, upon his death, it created a power vacuum. His empire spanned such a vast territory that no one could easily step into power over it all. So, as soon as Alexander died, his generals began to battle for whatever territory they could claim.

One general who rose to power in this period was Seleucus. At first, Seleucus gained control of northern Palestine (northern Israel) and the land that used to make up the Persian Empire. Eventually, his descendants, called the Seleucids, took control of the entire Holy Land. And as they did, things really began to change for the Jewish people.

Whereas Alexander had enforced Greek culture throughout his empire, the Seleucids took this to the extreme. They aggressively and violently imposed Hellenism upon the Jewish people in unprecedented ways. They required them to embrace Greek culture and worship Greek gods. By itself, this was enough to spark resistance and frustration among the Jewish people—many of these practices were directly in conflict with God's commands. But what the Seleucids did next was worse.

In addition to imposing Greek culture, the Seleucids attempted to eliminate the Jewish religion. They appointed their own men to the position of high priest over Israel and later made it a capital offense to practice Judaism. Jews were not even allowed to circumcise their sons or own a copy of the Torah. The final straw was when the Seleucids desecrated the temple in Jerusalem by erecting a statue of Zeus in the temple and sacrificing a pig on the altar.

This sparked the Maccabean revolt. The Jews rose up and went to war to throw out the Seleucids. Afterward, the Jews cleansed and rededicated the temple to God (this event is still celebrated today as Hanukkah) and resumed their religious practices with passion and fervor. When Jesus began his ministry, these sentiments were still strong. The people had been prevented from observing the Torah for far too long; they would not take it for granted.

Shabbat was a custom that held special importance within the Jewish community at this time. People paid careful attention to the customs and practices associated with this sacred day. They prepared certain foods, spoke specific prayers, and were meticulous about obeying God's command to rest.

In fact, at that time, rabbis distinguished thirty-nine *melachot* (pronounced *meh-lah-khot*), or categories of labor, that were to be prohibited on the Sabbath. They believed it was essential that people return to proper observance of the Torah. Prohibiting people from engaging in these thirty-nine categories of labor was an attempt to ensure that they did so.

Nevertheless, while the rabbis' intentions may have been good, their practices were questionable. Episode 2 highlights a fictionalized idea that Nicodemus, a prominent religious leader himself, becomes concerned about the atmosphere surrounding Shabbat. He feels that in their fervor, the Jewish religious leaders and people have become distracted, and such distractions are not only harming their relationship with the Lord; they are also harming their relationships with one another.

For instance, while Shabbat is supposed to be a time of communing with the Lord, many Jews seem to be more concerned about who will be in attendance at their weekly Shabbat meal. Jesus himself spoke of this in Luke's gospel.

> When Jesus noticed that all who had come to the dinner were trying to sit in the seats of honor near the head of the table, he gave them this advice: "When you are invited to a wedding feast, don't sit in the seat of honor. What if someone who is more distinguished than you has also been invited? The host will come and say, 'Give this person your seat.'

Then you will be embarrassed, and you will have to take whatever seat is left at the foot of the table!

"Instead, take the lowest place at the foot of the table. Then when your host sees you, he will come and say, 'Friend, we have a better place for you!' Then you will be honored in front of all the other guests. For those who exalt themselves will be humbled, and those who humble themselves will be exalted." (14:7–11 NLT)

Through this teaching, we get a glimpse into the dining customs of Jesus' day. Table seating mattered. The head of the table was the seat of honor, and every guest wanted to be the one given the most honor. Failing that, each tried to get as close as possible to the one who was most honored. In an honor/shame culture like this one, honor was transferable. So, to be near the one who was most honored meant that you too would be more highly honored. We see this reflected in the episode when a couple who enters Nicodemus's house quietly conspires to "try to get a seat at the head of the table."

Jesus, however, instructs people to do the opposite. Rather than seeking the seat of greatest honor, he commands his followers to prefer the lowest, humblest position. Jesus himself sits in a place of humility in the episode.

The Shabbat table Jesus joins, the one hosted by Mary (no longer Lilith), looks quite different from Nicodemus's. There are no religious leaders or people of prominence present. Around this table are the blind, the poor, and the outcast. No one is fighting to get to the head of Mary's table. No one's status is being improved by their attendance.

Here, the only thing that matters is that the people of God are gathered in the presence of the Lord.

But the significance of these two Shabbat meals goes beyond just the identities of the people present. The filmmakers also want us to notice the customs being practiced. In fact, it is in these customs that each element of this episode—Matthew's dedication to his dominus, Nicodemus's questions about Jesus, and the Shabbat prayers of their ancestors—come together.

At both Shabbat meals, there is a cup present. This cup would have been filled with wine, and as people drank from it, they would have prayed a prayer called the *kiddush* (pronounced *kee-doosh*). Mary prays it in this episode.

> Blessed are you, Lord God, ruler of the universe, who creates the fruit of the vine; you have lovingly and willingly given us your Shabbat as an inheritance in memory of creation, because it is the first day of our holy assemblies in memory of the exodus from Egypt. Blessed are you, Lord our God, King of the universe, who brings forth bread from the earth.[1]

The kiddush was a prayer of thanksgiving, praising God for the fruit of the vine. Since wine was associated with celebration and rejoicing over the blessings of the Lord, the kiddush was intended to help people remember all that God had done for them. It was a prayer they would have prayed every week throughout their lives.

The kiddush wasn't reserved for Shabbat only, though. It was also prayed during the Passover seder meal. And on one particular Passover, years after the events of this episode, this familiar prayer would take on an entirely new meaning for Jesus' disciples.

During the last meal Jesus shared with his disciples, as they were sharing wine and praying the kiddush, we can imagine Jesus looking at his disciples and saying, "Whenever you drink this, remember me." In other words, "Remember who I am. Remember what I am about to do for you. Remember what all of this means." For it was on that night, after Jesus had shared that cup with them, that he was put on trial, and on the very next day, he was crucified.

Jesus knew that after he was gone, people would wonder what it all meant. Who was Jesus, really? What was he truly here to do? He knew that as time wore on, memories would fade, lies would spread, and it would be even more important for his followers to remember. So Jesus pointed them to the cup and to the kiddush. He told them that on every future Shabbat, when they came together to share these things, they should remember him, and they should remember what all of this means.

No matter what is happening around them, this will be their reminder that Jesus is Lord. He is their Savior, their dominus. God walked among them. They ate with him, prayed with him, lived alongside him. They watched him die and saw him rise again. They witnessed proof that all these things were true, and it was vital that they remember.

Eventually, Rome would fade away. No longer would the Jews be under the heel of Roman legions. But this didn't mean that the battle for their hearts would be over. There would always be something or someone seeking to be their lord.

Shabbat presents a powerful opportunity for Jewish believers. Just as it reminded their ancestors of the God who liberated them from slavery, it will remind them of the Savior who has freed them from sin.

It does the same for us today.

Shabbat is an opportunity to ask ourselves: Who truly is my Lord? Am I fully surrendered to Jesus, or am I still holding something back? Am I truly trusting him to be my Savior, or am I still trying to save myself?

Let me ask you: Where in your life are you working tirelessly to resolve all of your problems, when what you truly need to do is rest and trust Jesus?

Where do you need to remember what Jesus has done in your life so that you might have faith in what he has yet to do?

Because what God asked the Israelites to do at Mount Sinai is the same thing Jesus asks us to do from the cross: Trust in me. Put your faith in me and me alone. Let me be your Lord.

And I will give you rest.

Episode 3

SIGNS

When the Pharisees and Sadducees came to test him,
they asked him to show them a sign from heaven.

—Matt. 16:1

So they said to him, "Then what sign will you perform,
so that we can see it and believe you? What will you do?"

—John 6:30

S how us a sign!

Throughout his ministry, Jesus was faced with this demand. The Pharisees wanted a miraculous sign from heaven. The crowd who had just witnessed Jesus' miracle of loaves and fishes asked for still another sign in order to believe in him—as if the miracle itself weren't enough!

This need for signs reflects their lack of faith. They require empirical evidence, visible proof. In many ways, they have been taught to think like this. They have read the prophecies. They have listened to their rabbis. They know what they are looking for in the Messiah, and they require proof that Jesus is indeed the fulfillment of these things.

The irony, though, is that there are signs all around them. Jesus fulfills dozens of prophecies. But are these the signs they are looking for?

In episode 3, the focus is on the relationship between Jesus and children. But there is actually a much deeper message unfolding. As we listen to their conversations and observe their interactions, we get a clearer picture of both the signs that people were looking for as they awaited the Messiah and the source from which those expectations were coming.

Ultimately, we must ask ourselves: What would I have believed? What would have convinced me? Would I have been one with the crowds?

Or would my faith have been like that of a child, one for whom the signs were obvious and the decision easy?

Chapter 9

JESUS GOES CAMPING

Somewhere along the outskirts of Capernaum, there is a camp. It is a lonely, solitary place. A simple tent stands next to a small fire and an assortment of tools. This is the temporary residence of a bachelor, a traveler with no place that he can truly call home.

It belongs to Jesus.

This is the screenwriters' speculation, of course, as is this entire episode. There is no biblical record of these events, but they provide insight into the compassion and humanity of the Lord.

When Jesus appears on-screen in this episode, it is obvious that he is struggling. While he might enjoy the peace of being alone amid God's creation, his heart aches over the burden that he alone must carry.

In many ways, this is like Jesus' later experience in the garden of Gethsemane before his crucifixion. There is a task before him that no one else can execute. It is a task of great importance, and the pressure is overwhelming.

So often, it is easy for us to focus almost exclusively on Jesus'
divine nature, how he is God in the flesh, living among us. But this
opening scene reminds us that just as Jesus is fully divine, he is also
fully human. He must have endured stress and managed emotions in
much the same way that we do.

What the filmmakers want us to glimpse here is the heaviness of
the task before Jesus on the threshold of his ministry. It is one thing for
him to know what is about to unfold; it is another to execute it.

But Jesus is residing in these woods for more than just solitary
prayer and reflection. This campsite is a foretaste of the life he will be
living over the next few years.

Throughout the Gospels, we consistently see Jesus addressed by
the title rabbi. This is a Hebrew word that can be translated "teacher."
But this translation does little to truly reflect the life and importance
of a rabbi in the first century.

When we hear the word teacher today, we tend to think of someone who passes along information. The teacher has information, and
the student needs it, making the relationship very transactional. In
fact, in many cases, there doesn't even need to be much of a relationship between a student and teacher for education to occur.

The relationship between a rabbi (teacher) and a disciple (student)
at the time of Jesus, however, was much different. The rabbi–disciple
relationship was close and intimate. Disciples left everything to follow
their rabbi. They trusted his every word, followed his every command,
and dedicated themselves to becoming just like him. This relationship
was so close, in fact, that it was said to rival the relationship between a
father and a son.

This is the level of trust and intimacy that Jesus will have with
those he calls to be his disciples. And this temporary campsite is a

glimpse into how they will spend much of their time with him over the next few years.

The life of some rabbis of the era was one of itinerancy. Such a rabbi would travel from town to town, spreading his unique interpretation of the Torah. He was not paid for this work but instead relied on the charity of those in the towns he visited.

During certain seasons, a rabbi would rest from his travels and his disciples would return to their families. He might spend this time studying the Torah, or he might return to a family trade.[1] This is, in fact, what we see Jesus doing at his campsite in this imagined scenario. He is carving items that he intends to offer for sale. Scripture tells us that Jesus and his father, Joseph, were both *tektons*. This is the Greek word for a carpenter or stonemason. Jesus would have been a craftsman who knew how to work with a variety of tools and mediums.

So, while the life of an itinerant rabbi may have been esteemed, it was not necessarily glamorous. At times, it could be a life of survival, relying on God and the hospitality of others for food, shelter, and other basic needs. And since this was the way the rabbi lived, his disciples were expected to do the same.

In Luke's gospel, Jesus told his disciples to embrace this lifestyle when he sent them out to preach, heal, and cast out demons: "Take nothing for the journey—no staff, no bag, no bread, no money, no extra shirt. Whatever house you enter, stay there until you leave that town. If people do not welcome you, leave their town and shake the dust off your feet as a testimony against them" (9:3–5 NIV). These instructions weren't intended to make the disciples struggle unnecessarily. Jesus was simply describing the life of a rabbi and instructing his disciples to live as he did.

And yet, while Jesus is addressed as a rabbi and functions as one, he has not come to that position in the traditional way. Usually, a rabbi would go through years of formal education and training. But John's gospel tells us, "The people were surprised when they heard him. 'How does he know so much when he hasn't been trained?' they asked" (7:15 NLT).

Jesus didn't study under another rabbi or go to the school of higher education, called *Bet Midrash* (pronounced *bayt-mee-drahsh*). As far as we know, Jesus simply learned his father's trade and then embarked upon his ministry. Even the people of Nazareth, his hometown, were amazed at his wisdom and understanding when he taught in their synagogue (Mark 6:1–3).

If people were searching for a Messiah, the signs certainly did not seem to be pointing to Jesus. While he might have been a religious teacher, and while there may have been rumors that he had performed amazing spiritual acts, he was not what the people were looking for. When it came to the Messiah, people were expecting someone more like a young David before he became king—leading the armies of Israel in battle to throw off the reign of the oppressor. Jesus did not fit that description.

In our day, centuries removed from the events, it is hard for us to understand the severity of this dilemma for those who were encountering Jesus for the first time. When reading the Bible, one of the hardest things for us to do is to set aside what we already believe about Jesus and to ask ourselves, "What *would* I have believed?"

What would I have thought of Jesus if I had met him on the dusty roads of Israel? Would I have recognized him as the Messiah I had been waiting for all my life? Or would he have appeared to be just another rabbi, a simple traveler like so many others? Even if I understood him to be from God, would I allow myself to believe in him if he didn't seem to be the sort of Messiah the religious leaders had been describing?

What would it have taken to convince me? And based on what I see in Scripture, would I have truly been convinced?

> When reading the Bible, one of the hardest things for us to do is to set aside what we already believe about Jesus and to ask ourselves, "What *would* I have believed?"

While we might feel guilty in responding to these questions with any answer but yes, there is value in honest wrestling. Our belief in Jesus is never something we should take for granted. We must reclaim our faith each and every day.

As this episode begins, we are invited once again to look at the signs and ask ourselves: "What would I have made of it all?"

Chapter 10

A CHILD'S FIRST PRAYER

What was the first prayer you ever learned? Was it a blessing you prayed over each meal? A prayer from the hymnal at church? Or like me, did you lie in bed each night, reciting this oddly morbid children's prayer:

> Now I lay me down to sleep,
> I pray the Lord my soul to keep.
> And if I die before I wake,
> I pray the Lord my soul to take.

And we wonder why we all had nightmares!

In episode 3, we encounter a variety of prayers. Jesus prays a blessing over his food. Later, he joins with the children to sing Psalm 133. And eventually, he listens as the children recite a prayer that stands above the rest, a prayer that most certainly would have been the first prayer that he and each of these children ever learned: the Shema.

The Shema was the most important of all Jewish prayers. It was recited twice a day, every day. The words, like many Jewish prayers, came directly from Scripture:

> Hear, O Israel: The LORD our God, the LORD is one. Love the LORD your God with all your heart and with all your soul and with all your strength. These commandments that I give you today are to be on your hearts. Impress them on your children. Talk about them when you sit at home and when you walk along the road, when you lie down and when you get up. Tie them as symbols on your hands and bind them on your foreheads. Write them on the doorframes of your houses and on your gates. (Deut. 6:4–9 NIV)

As we've seen, this prayer is called the Shema because of the Hebrew word that begins the prayer: *shema*, which means "hear." From Scripture, we know that this prayer was incredibly important to Jesus. When asked to select the greatest of all the commandments in the Torah, Jesus begins with the Shema, saying, "'You shall love the Lord your God with all your heart and with all your soul and with all your mind.' This is the greatest and first commandment" (Matt. 22:37–38).

> "First, it is a Semitic hyperbole that exaggerates a contrast so that it can be seen more clearly. 'Hate' (μισέω miseō) does not mean anger or hostility. It indicates that if there is a conflict, one's response to the demands of discipleship must take precedence over even the most sacred of human relationships. … There is no duty higher than commitment to Jesus and to being his disciple."[1] – R. Alan Culpepper

To understand why Jesus would select this of all commands, and why it was so important within the Jewish community, we first have to understand what it means. The Shema is more than a command to really, really love God. Each part of this command reflects a different aspect of our love for God.

For instance, the word for love itself is the Hebrew word *ahav* (pronounced *ah-hahv*). But unlike our modern understanding of love, *ahav* isn't describing a feeling; it's describing an action. In Hebrew culture, love was understood in terms of choice: to love something was to choose it, and to hate something was to not choose it.[2]

This explains other moments in Scripture, such as when Jesus tells his disciples that to follow him, they must hate their parents, wives, children, and even themselves (see Luke 14:26). He isn't talking about a *feeling* of hatred. He's telling them that they must love (choose) him over everyone else.[3]

In the same way, the Shema prayer is God's command that the Hebrew people choose him above all other gods. Each day, they will be tempted and lured away by the world around them. So, each day, they must remind themselves to choose the Lord.

The language Jesus would have spoken (and even the original languages of the Gospels) is much debated. Many believe Mishnaic Hebrew, similar to Aramaic, was commonly spoken at the time. There's also evidence from the early church fathers that Matthew's gospel was originally written in Hebrew (something Matthew would only do if Hebrew were a commonly understood language). So, while we might have these words recorded only in Greek, it is most likely they were originally spoken in Aramaic or some form of Hebrew. Either way, the Hebrew mindset is really what matters most. What's significant is the Jews' idea of "love" and "hate" regardless of what words they used.

But the act of loving and choosing God is multifaceted. The Lord says that his people must love God with all their "heart." This is the Hebrew word *lev* (pronounced *layv*). And just like ahav, lev means something different from what we expect in Western culture.

For us, the heart is the seat of our emotions; it is where our feelings reside. But this is not the case in Jewish culture. To Jews, the heart is where the mind resides; it is where one's thoughts come from. So, to love God with your entire heart means to love God with your every thought.

> In Hebrew culture, love was understood in terms of choice: to love something was to choose it, and to hate something was to not choose it.

God then commands that the Hebrew people love the Lord with their entire "soul." This is the Hebrew word *nephesh* (pronounced *neh'-fesh*). And rather than describing the soul as a spirit that lives within us, nephesh is used to describe a person's entire life. To love the Lord with your nephesh means that you love God with every facet of your life. Where you go, what you do, how you live—all of these are opportunities to exercise your devotion to the Lord.

The final command that God gives in the Shema is for people to love the Lord with all their "strength." This is the Hebrew word *m'eod* (pronounced *meh-ode*). It is a difficult word to translate. It literally means all of your "very." Basically, it is a command to love the Lord with every ounce of energy you have.

So, when God commands that we love the Lord with our heart, our soul, and our strength, and when he tells us that this is the greatest commandment, he is not saying that we must simply *feel* an abundance of love for God. God is saying that we must demonstrate our love through our actions, through every thought that crosses our minds, in every facet of our lives, and with every ounce of energy that we have.

In the episode, as Jesus hears the children reciting these words, he is visibly moved by their profession of faith. Because, for Jesus, this is a sign of the coming kingdom. The kingdom that he came here to build is one in which people do not merely recite the Shema—they embody it. It is a kingdom where the hearts of all people return to the Lord.

The passion and understanding of these children fill Jesus with hope. At the beginning of the episode, we watch as he wrestles with the weight of the task before him. But soon after, these children demonstrate that there are already those whose hearts are ready to receive him and the message he brings.

As followers of Jesus, we should rejoice in this moment as well. The faith of these children is a reflection of the faith we long to see in our own children and in the future generations that surround us. It is a glimpse of the kingdom rooted in a prayer.

Perhaps we too should begin and end each day with the Shema, reminding ourselves daily of who God is, who we are, and who God has called us to be.

Perhaps for us it could be a sign, a point we look to each day that keeps us centered and grounded in our faith no matter what the world might throw at us.

Indeed, this has been its very intention from the start. For in God's own words:

Listen, Israel, and carefully obey these laws. Then
all will go well for you, and you will become a great
nation in a fertile land, just as the LORD, the God of
your ancestors, has promised you. Listen, people of
Israel! The LORD our God is the only LORD. Love
the LORD your God with all your heart, all your
soul, and all your strength. Always remember these
commands I give you today. Teach them to your children, and talk about them when you sit at home and
walk along the road, when you lie down and when
you get up. Write them down and tie them to your
hands as a sign. Tie them on your forehead to remind
you, and write them on your doors and gates. (Deut.
6:3–9 NCV)

Chapter 11

WE WANT A KING!

When Jewish children are born, their parents face a very important decision: What do we name this child?

It's more than simply trying to find a name that is pleasing to the ear. It isn't a matter of selecting a name that is trendy or avoiding a name that reminds them of an ex-boyfriend. In Judaism, a name is connected to a child's character and story.

We see this consistently throughout Scripture. The name Moses (or Moshe) means to "draw out," a reference to his experiences in life. Judas (or Judah) means "Let God be praised," a picture of who his parents hoped he would become.

The same is true for Jesus.

As the children gather to spend time with Jesus one day, we learn that one of these children actually shares the same name as Jesus: Joshua. Both names come from the Hebrew name *Yehoshua*, whose shortened form is *Yeshua*. It is a name that means "God is salvation." Jesus' very name prophesies who he will become and what he has come here to do.

Jesus will bring *God's salvation* to his people!

> *Y'shuah* is the Hebrew word that means "salvation." The *yeho* at the beginning of *Yehoshua* is a form of the word *Yah*, which is the word for God.

What is not as obvious is how Jesus will do this. For when people look upon Jesus, they do not see many indications that he is the Messiah they have been expecting.

At the time of Jesus, many people were eagerly awaiting the Messiah. The children in this episode comment on how their rabbi has been teaching them about the Messiah. Rabbi Josiah has told them to expect a great military leader who will lead the people in battle against the Romans.

This was the most common expectation about the Messiah at the time of Jesus. Almost all of the would-be messiahs who came before and after Jesus were military leaders who promised to remove Rome from the Holy Land. Men like Theudas, Simon of Perea, and Judas of Galilee drew many followers and led them in armed uprisings against their Roman occupiers.[1] (For Theudas and Judas of Galilee, see Acts 5:36–37.) And even though they each were defeated, people continued to hold out hope for a great military leader. They believed that Scripture prophesied that the Messiah would be a "Son of David," who would, like David, be a warrior king who would drive Israel's enemies from the land.

It is no surprise, then, that many people dismissed Jesus as a possible Messiah. He did not fit the profile. Even though he performed miracles, was gifted in interpreting the Scriptures, and drew a massive following, he was, as far as they could tell, neither warrior nor king.

Furthermore, his message seemed to be the opposite of that which they thought the Messiah would preach. Rather than leading his people in a war cry against Rome, Jesus said, "Blessed are the peacemakers"

(Matt. 5:9) and commanded that his followers "turn the other [cheek]" (v. 39). This may even explain why the Gospels tell us that Jesus' own family struggled to believe in him. He didn't match the signs, and he didn't meet their expectations.

But as the children listen to Jesus, they learn that his vision of salvation is far grander than the one they've been taught to expect. The salvation he's bringing isn't just for a select group of people in one location at one moment in history. He's coming so that God's kingdom might reign on earth, so that God will rule in people's hearts, and so that the words of the Shema might be brought to fruition in their lives.

If people are willing to look for these things, they will see that the signs are obvious. Everywhere Jesus will go, the sick will be healed, the sinful will be transformed, and God's Word will spread. Spiritual renewal is going to occur throughout Israel. Even Gentiles will come to know the Lord.

What the Lord is teaching both the children and us is the importance of embracing Jesus for who he is rather than judging him against who we expect him to be. It is far too easy, even for Christians, to judge Jesus by our own criteria. We are tempted to believe that he should make our lives easier, prosper us greatly, and ask from us only that which we want to be asked.

But a true disciple says, "Lord, make me into your image. Shape me into who you want me to be. And do through me whatever you desire to do." As disciples, it is our mission to discover who Jesus is and what he desires and to shape our lives around those things.

This is what the children do each day when they come to visit Jesus. Their sole desires are to join him in his work and to learn. They are satisfied with simply being in his presence. They have no expectations or qualifications by which they intend to judge him. Their decision has already been made: they will trust him. Now their focus is to simply obey and learn.

How beautiful would it be if this were how we all approached Jesus! If we didn't require signs and proofs, but simply trusted and obeyed.

How much more might we grow if our focus each day were on following Jesus, doing whatever he called us to do, and going wherever he called us to go?

> We are tempted to believe that he should make our lives easier, prosper us greatly, and ask from us only that which we want to be asked.
>
> But a true disciple says, "Lord, make me into your image. Shape me into who you want me to be. And do through me whatever you desire to do."

What might it look like to live with such passion that we devoted the same energy to spending time with Jesus in God's Word as we would if he were standing physically present before us?

Indeed, this is happening all around us. We just have to look for the signs.

And perhaps the first place we should look for these signs is in our children.

Chapter 12

GIRL POWER!

After spending several days with Jesus, a young girl named Abigail excitedly approaches his tent, hoping to encounter him once again. But this time, rather than finding Jesus as she has earlier in the episode, she finds a gift. Left for her where his campsite used to be is a miniature stable with horses and a manger.

There is also a sign that says, "Abigail, I know you can read. You are very special. This is for you. I did not come only for the wealthy."

In just four short sentences, *The Chosen* reveals important insights not only about Abigail but also about Jesus.

Throughout the episode, it has been clear that Abigail stands out among her peers. She is the first to encounter Jesus and is quick to invite her friends to meet him. Her ability to understand the Torah rivals that of the boys in her group, which is especially outstanding given that she has had no formal education.

While young boys would begin their religious education at around age six, girls were educated at home. They learned Scripture from their parents, attended synagogue each week, and gleaned much of their understanding from the Jewish practice of naturally weaving Scripture throughout daily life. The Shema commanded parents, "Impress [these commands] on your children. Talk about them when you sit at home and when you walk along the road, when you lie down and when you get up" (Deut. 6:7 NIV). So, even tasks as familiar as doing laundry and preparing meals would have been opportunities for girls to learn and reflect on God's Word.

Additionally, while girls might not attend Torah school, they did have many opportunities to participate in the religious life of the community. Women could be counted as part of the ten persons required for certain prayers to be spoken. They participated in religious debates and could even study with rabbis.[1] For instance, in Luke's gospel, Mary, unlike her sister, Martha, is said to have "sat at the Lord's feet listening to what he said" (10:39 NIV). To sit at a rabbi's feet meant that you were studying under that rabbi. It wasn't a matter of listening from the sidelines. This was active participation.

> "Women were encouraged to sit in on the advanced discussions at the synagogue if they were able. A few even acquired the high-level education required to contribute to rabbinic debates, and their words are still on record. Some restrictions on women, like separating men and women during worship, actually arose several centuries later."
> — Ann Spangler and Lois Tverberg

But what makes Abigail special is not just that she has learned Torah but that she understands it. This is why Jesus gives her this gift and leaves her this sign. She has demonstrated that she knows what he is here to do and embraces his message.

In fact, Jesus' note to her reveals what that message is: he is not here for the rich only.

This recalls a moment in Luke's gospel when John the Baptist sends his disciples to ask Jesus if he is indeed the Messiah. Jesus responds, "Go and tell John what you have seen and heard: the blind receive sight, the lame walk, lepers are cleansed, the deaf hear; the dead are raised, the poor have good news announced to them" (7:22).

In other words, go back and tell John about the miracles you have seen.

It's enough of a sign that Jesus is performing miracles. But the signs Jesus is describing are prophecies that have come true!

When Jesus makes references to the blind walking, the deaf hearing, and the good news being proclaimed to the poor, he is describing prophecies from the book of Isaiah, such as, "In that day the deaf will hear the words of the scroll, and out of gloom and darkness the eyes of the blind will see" (29:18 NIV) and, "The Spirit of the Sovereign LORD is on me, because the LORD has anointed me to proclaim good news to the poor" (61:1 NIV).

Jesus himself references the latter prophecy when he preaches in Nazareth. He tells his hearers that this Scripture has been fulfilled in their hearing (see Luke 4:16–21). In other words, Jesus is telling them that he is the Messiah and has come to fulfill this prophecy. He has come not for the rich only, but also for the poor.

Jesus tells the congregation in Nazareth that he had come to "proclaim the year of the LORD's favor" (v. 19 NIV), which is another quotation from Isaiah 61. His audience would have understood this as a reference to the Year of Jubilee. This is a special year that came every fifty years, as outlined in Leviticus 25, when God's people did not work their farms or vineyards but relied entirely on the Lord for food. It was also a year in which slaves were freed, the poor were supported, and people were redeemed from their dire circumstances. God gives detailed instructions for how those with means and power must assist those without.

This is what Jesus is describing in his final sentence to Abigail on the sign. He is describing the Jubilee that he is ushering in. Through Jesus, God's commands in Leviticus 25 will be fulfilled. Those who follow him will embody what God commanded in those verses.

While the religious leaders will be looking for signs of a conquering king, Jesus declares that the true signs of the Messiah are already before them. God's redemptive plan is unfolding, and Jesus is at the center of it.

It is important for followers of Jesus to remember that this has not changed, even centuries later. The signs of the kingdom were not only for those living in first-century Israel. They surround each of us every day.

Daily, we are confronted with signs and reminders to join Jesus in his work. We too encounter those who are in need of relief. And we are posed with the same question Jesus set before Abigail and the children:

Will you join me?

Episode 4

FISHING

Aday journeying northward through Israel is as surprising as it is exciting. As your day begins, you find yourself in the oppressive heat of the Negev desert. Riverbeds are dry. Life is scarce. The palette of the terrain seems to be limited to shades of red and brown.

And yet, the land has a unique beauty. Animals and vegetation find ways to survive. The presence of God is palpable, a reminder of the many biblical stories in which God sustained his people in this region.

From there, the terrain becomes challenging in a new way. The flat desert transitions into rolling hills and deep valleys. To the west is the Mediterranean Sea, and rising in the east is the mountaintop city of Jerusalem.

Life is more abundant here, but water is still limited. Living things survive because of the runoff from the Jordan River. It is the lifeblood that sustains the people who reside here and the crops and animals they depend on for survival. Outside this fertile area, there are little more than dry riverbeds, a hidden oasis here or there, and a salty sea.

If you continue north, though, making your way toward the uppermost portion of Israel, you will find a spot unique from anything you've passed along the way: the Sea of Galilee.

For the earliest nomads making their way through this region, the Sea of Galilee must have felt like a gift from heaven. This is a freshwater lake teeming with life. The land around it is relatively lush and abundant.

Surprisingly, though, while Galilee may be rich in resources, at the time of Jesus, it was not rich in stature. Many have wondered why Jesus chose to establish his ministry in Galilee, a rural region whose people spoke with a noticeable accent. Why not focus on Jerusalem, the home of the temple and the center of religious activity?

But as we have seen, what Galilee might have lacked in prestige, it made up for in other ways. The Via Maris, the primary trade route through Israel, came nowhere close to Jerusalem but ran right alongside the Sea of Galilee. This thriving trade route brought travelers from various nations, exposure to new ideas, and an abundance of money. This made Galilee the perfect place to start a global movement.

When Jesus began to preach his message of the coming kingdom, he was speaking to a community both rooted in the traditions of Judaism and constantly exposed to new ideas and trends. They were primed for change.

So, as Jesus looks out upon the Sea of Galilee, watching men cast their nets into the water, paying close attention to two brothers who appear particularly stressed, he is certain that this is the perfect place to go "fishing."

Chapter 13

EMPTY NETS

As far back as they can remember, Simon and Andrew have never known much of anything beyond the Sea of Galilee. From their childhood home in Bethsaida to their current residence in Capernaum, the freshwater lake has always been the first thing they smell when they awake and the last thing they see outside their windows as they fall asleep.

They were fishermen, members of a trade that, while not particularly esteemed, was vital to the region. Fish was a regular part of the Mediterranean diet, and it was consumed, sold, and traded throughout Galilee and beyond.

The Sea of Galilee itself has long been known for several varieties of fish. The most common is *Tilapia galileia*. This is commonly referred to as "Saint Peter's Fish." It is a flavorful white fish that is still served in restaurants along the Sea of Galilee today.

Then there are barbels. These members of the carp family are known for the barbs in the corners of their mouths. They are frequently used for Shabbat meals and other Jewish feasts.[1]

Finally, there are sardines. Though the smallest of the commercial fish, they make up about half of the fish caught in the Sea of Galilee each year. They are often pickled or preserved in some other fashion. At the time of Jesus, they would have been salted and processed in Magdala, the largest source of preserved fish along the Galilee.[2]

To catch each of these kinds of fish, fishermen would use a variety of techniques. The primary means of commercial fishing was the drag-net. This is the method being used by Simon, Andrew, James, John, and Zebedee at the end of episode 4. Two boats would be situated parallel to shore. A weighted net would then be cast into the water between the boats, resting along the floor of the sea. As the boats headed toward the shore, the net would drag along the bottom, capturing all the fish in its path. This type of fishing would gather massive hauls, sometimes requiring up to sixteen men to process the catch.

Next, there was the cast net. This is the technique Simon uses in the episode when he fishes alone in the boat. To fish this way, a fisher-man would toss a small net, weighted on its outer circumference, into the water. After it sank to the bottom, he would dive into the water to cinch the net and raise the entire catch to the surface.

Finally, there was the trammel net. This was similar to the drag-net in that it was spread out over a wide area and weighted to the seafloor. Rather than being one long net, however, a trammel net was composed of three different nets joined together. The outer nets were made of large mesh, while the middle net had much smaller mesh. Once the net was set in place, men on the outer edges of the nets beat oars against the water, scaring fish toward the middle of the nets. In the midst of the frenzy, the nets were dragged to shore, trapping the fish between the various layers.

In general, most fishing would take place at night. The dark waters would disguise the nets, making it easier to gather large hauls.

Fishermen would set out in the evening and return to shore in the morning.

After turning over their catch to be sold, they would clean and mend their nets for the next night. This practice was essential, since unclean nets could dry out or rot, and torn nets could let fish escape. Without good nets, the men could not catch fish.

Just as important as a fisherman's net was his boat, which was essential for dragging the nets into the water and fishing in the deeper parts of the sea. Unfortunately for Simon and Andrew, as imagined in episode 4, there is a likelihood that they will lose their boat. Their tax debt has grown so high that Rome is threatening to confiscate their possessions—including their boat, their only means of income—to settle the debt.

Faced with such grim prospects, it is clear that Simon is willing to do anything to fix this situation. Lie to his wife? Betray his friends? Break the Sabbath? He seems to feel that everything is an option when so much is at stake.

Have you ever found yourself in a situation like this: saddled with a dilemma that tempts you to compromise your integrity, perhaps even harming those around you, to protect yourself?

In a way, this situation is similar to fishing. As fishermen set up the trammel net, the fish are perfectly safe. They are calm and aware of their surroundings. But as the oars strike the water, things quickly change. Rather than fleeing to safety, the fish, caught up in the frenzy, actually swim into the very heart of danger.

As Jesus watches Simon, he sees a fish in frenzy heading straight toward danger. Simon is confused and scared. He recognizes the threat in front of him but seems helpless to turn away. He is racing blindly into the darkness, putting at risk those who are closest to him.

Thankfully, Jesus is a fisher of men. He knows how to handle a fish in frenzy. Soon, Jesus will offer Simon a way out of the trap. And in doing so, he will free not only Simon but also those who are caught in the net with him.

Chapter 14

A HOLY SHOUTING MATCH

Is it okay to shout at God?

Have you ever wondered about this? Are we allowed to be angry with God? Does God get upset when we vent our frustration in his direction? At what point have we gone too far?

As Simon stands in his boat, exhausted after hours of fishing with nothing to show for it, he is even more distraught over the hopelessness of his situation, so he cries out to God in anger and frustration.

In the first few episodes of *The Chosen*, we observe that while Simon is deeply rooted in his Jewish faith, his relationship with God is not as strong as it once was. Not only is he tempted to break the Sabbath and ignore the Torah, but also he seems to hold God responsible for the terrible situation in which he finds himself.

At the height of his frustration, Simon mocks God's promise to Abraham that God would "multiply [his] descendants like the stars of heaven" (Gen. 26:4). He recounts how, instead of blessing his nation, God let them suffer. In the centuries that followed, God's people were enslaved by Egypt, exiled in Babylon, and conquered by Rome. Simon feels that God has abandoned his people and abandoned him.

He's not the only one.

Through Simon's anger, we actually catch a glimpse of a much wider frustration roiling at the time of Jesus. This ire extended throughout the Jewish community. The events that Simon recalls—slavery, exile, and subjugation—were still raw in the memories of the Jewish people. God had promised to prosper them, yet they suffered.

In the past, the Jewish people had thought they understood the reason for this suffering. They had what is called a "Deuteronomistic mindset." This meant they believed that when they were faithful to God, they prospered, but when they disobeyed God, they suffered.

For a long time, this mindset made sense; Israel's behavior matched their outcome. But after a while, they no longer saw the correlation. They were trying desperately to obey God, but their suffering continued.

This incongruency led people to consider new theories about God's presence in their situation and what it would take for God to save them. Some developed an apocalyptic mindset, a belief that the world was in the midst of an epic battle between good and evil. They believed their suffering meant that evil had taken root in the world but that God would reign victorious in the end.

Others, like the Pharisees, believed that the situation before them was a matter of sin. Even though the people were trying to be faithful, they weren't succeeding. Sin was still too prevalent. This caused the Pharisees to enact strict requirements pertaining to the Torah. Not only were people required to observe all of God's written laws; they were also required to observe all the oral traditions. In some cases, the Pharisees even added requirements to the oral traditions, making them overly strict in hopes that people would be protected from even accidentally breaking God's laws.

As we saw earlier, groups like the Zealots and the Essenes took different approaches. Zealots believed that God's people were being weak and need to fight for their freedom, joining God in expelling their foreign oppressors. Essenes, on the other hand, left society, preferring to create a faithful community free from the sinful behavior of many of their Jewish brethren.

Nevertheless, what all these groups held in common was their certainty that God was not helping them, and something must be done to remedy the situation. They lived with a mixture of guilt and frustration. And in Simon, we see firsthand what can happen when such combustible feelings finally erupt.

But Simon is certainly not the first person to shout at God. The Psalms are filled with moments of frustration when the psalmist questioned why God was allowing him to experience such pain and suffering. There is never the sense that he will be judged for this; God can handle our emotional outbursts.

In fact, an explosion of emotion can actually be an important part of our relationship with the Lord. Even Jesus vented his fear as he prayed to the Father on the eve of his crucifixion. He did not pretend that everything was fine or constrain the legitimate feelings welling up inside him. He confessed them honestly. But note that in the end he surrendered himself to his Father's will.

This is what Simon is doing as he shouts from his boat. He is scared, frustrated, and yearning for God's help. He releases every one of these thoughts and emotions. Then, once they are out in the open, he is finally ready to surrender.

Throughout the Gospels, Jesus "fished" for disciples. He searched for those who were ready, who were willing to surrender to him fully as their Lord and Savior. Often, it is the sick and broken who are the most eager to receive him, those who have lost hope, who can't rely on themselves or the power of others but are ready to submit themselves to the power of Jesus' name. These are the ones who experience true salvation.

Let me ask you: What parts of your life do you need to fully surrender to Jesus?

Do you need to vent your feelings and frustrations, freeing yourself to receive what only Jesus can offer? Where are you still trying to resolve things through your own strength and strategies, caught up in the frenzy and only heading deeper into the darkness?

I'd be surprised if any of us has not felt lost at some point in our lives. I know I have. But thankfully, two thousand years later, Jesus is still fishing, still searching for those who are ready to receive him. He can handle our fears and our frustrations. He understands our pain.

In the end, Jesus wants to offer us salvation that won't just come someday in the future, once this life is over. He wants to save us now, while we are still standing in our boats, afraid for our future, hanging onto the hope that, through him, things can change both now and forever.

Chapter 15

SITTING AT THE FEET OF THE RABBI

Good teachers know how to get through to their students. They know what analogies to use and what points will penetrate the deepest. They know what will capture their attention and what will lose it.

What might a good teacher do to get through to an audience living on the Sea of Galilee, half of whom are listening from their fishing boats?

A good teacher would tell a story about fish, of course.

As Jesus stands on the shoreline, he adopts the typical posture of a rabbi in the first century. Positioned in front of his students, he has them gather at his feet. His back is to the water so he can take advantage of the natural acoustics of the sea. For his lesson, he presents a parable.

The parable Jesus recites in this scene comes from chapter 13 of Matthew's gospel.

Again, the kingdom of heaven is like a dragnet that was thrown into the sea and gathered fish of every kind, which when it was filled they pulled to shore and sat down and collected the good fish into containers, but the bad they threw out. Thus it will be at the end of the age. The angels will go out and separate the evil from among the righteous and throw them into the fiery furnace. In that place there will be weeping and gnashing of teeth! (13:47–50)

Now, according to Scripture, Jesus did not preach this parable along the shore of the Sea of Galilee. He preached it inside a house in Capernaum soon after a lengthy seaside lesson. Nevertheless, by including this lesson in this scene, *The Chosen* is reminding us that Jesus did not necessarily preach each parable only once during his ministry. He very well may have taught these parables frequently. Comparing the gospel accounts reveals that these parables were often shared in different settings. Rather than assuming that the Gospels are in conflict, we can know that they reflect the frequency with which Jesus shared these invaluable lessons.

So, at some point, Jesus may have found himself along the shoreline, surrounded by a small crowd at his feet and fishermen listening from the boats behind him, as he told this parable.

This story would have caught his audience's attention for several reasons. First, Jesus mentions dragnets, the essential fishing tool we talked about in chapter 13. Perhaps this type of net was even sitting in fishermen's boats at that very moment. Then Jesus talks about a fiery furnace, a phrase that would have recalled to listeners' minds the story of Hananiah, Mishael, and Azariah (Shadrach, Meshach, and

Abednego) from the book of Daniel. Finally, all of this is contained within a parable about the kingdom of God, a vision of the salvation that Jesus is bringing to God's people.

As this story unfolds, the audience realizes that Jesus is presenting them with a choice. God's kingdom is coming, but not everyone will receive it. Just as Daniel's three friends were tested and proved their devotion to the Lord despite the cost, so we too will be tested. And the harsh reality is that only those who are ready to receive the kingdom will be able to experience it.

Naturally, the question that follows is: Am *I* ready to receive this kingdom?

This is the question Simon has been facing throughout the first several episodes. Without realizing it, Simon has been presented with a series of tests in which he has been forced to decide, "Will I trust the Lord, or will I put my hope somewhere else?"

But it is not Jesus' parable that convinces Simon. Rather, it is the way the parable comes to life.

At the conclusion of his lesson, Jesus instructs Simon to cast his net into the water once again. These seem like foolish instructions for several reasons. First, it is daytime, the worst time to fish with a dragnet. Second, Simon has been fishing all night with no success. Why would Jesus expect that a bountiful catch would suddenly appear now?

But it does! The catch is so great that it threatens to sink the boat. And in an instant, not only does Simon's situation improve; his resistance dissolves.

What Simon sees in Jesus is the hope he has been yelling at God about. Jesus is proof that God will provide. In this miracle, Simon gets a taste of the abundant nature of the kingdom of God. He sees salvation not just as a promise of some future hope but as something available right now.

When we think about salvation, there is a tendency to focus only on a future promise, the hope that when we die we will be saved for eternity in heaven. But when we look closer at Jesus' teachings, we realize that his promises are more often about the hope of salvation now.

The hungry will be satisfied. The sick will be healed. The captives will be freed.

And those who seek his kingdom will find it.

Like the fish in Jesus' parable, Simon is that catch Jesus has been hoping for. But unbeknownst to Simon, while the miracle he experienced that day will free him from his financial burdens, his decision to put his faith in Jesus will soon prove costlier than he ever imagined.

Chapter 16

LECH ACHARAI

Jesus often concluded his miracles by instructing the recipient to tell no one about what they had experienced. Some say this was because Jesus' time had not yet come and he did not want to reveal himself. Others suggest that this was so that he would not attract the attention of his opponents.

Both of these very well may be true. But I would like to suggest another reason. I believe that Jesus often tried to hide his miracles because miracles are a distraction.

For instance, in episode 4, it is natural to assume that the miracle of the fish is the central moment. After all of Simon's struggles, this event both removes his debt and opens his eyes to the truth about who Jesus is. But the most important moment in this episode isn't the miracle itself. It is something that happens soon after the miracle, something so subtle it is easy to overlook.

Simon jumps out of the boat and kneels before Jesus. Humbled and grateful, he is ready to believe that Jesus is indeed the Messiah. But rather than simply accepting Simon's faith, Jesus makes a request of him.

Jesus says, "Follow me."

Now, on the surface, it may appear that Jesus is simply inviting Simon to walk with him for a moment or even to travel alongside him for a time. But in these two words, Simon hears much more than a casual invitation. Jesus is asking Simon to make a tremendous sacrifice.

To understand this moment, it is important that we look at what has led up to it, something well outside of Simon's financial troubles and impetuous mistakes. This moment has been years in the making.

Around age six, every Jewish boy would begin his religious education. His parents would enroll him in a school called *Bet Sefer* (pronounced *bayt seh-fayr*), which means "House of the Book." For the next four years, he would devote himself to studying the Torah, especially books such as Genesis, Deuteronomy, and the Psalms. He would memorize vast portions of these books. There are even accounts of boys in Bet Sefer memorizing the first five books of the Bible in their entirety.

When a boy was around ten, the rabbis in charge would determine if he showed an aptitude for understanding the Scriptures. If he didn't, this would end his education and he would go on to learn his family trade. But if he was particularly gifted, he would proceed to the next level of education, called *Bet Talmud* (pronounced *bayt tahl-mood*).

Bet Talmud means "house of learning." And whereas a young boy would study the written Torah in Bet Sefer, in Bet Talmud he would begin to memorize the *Mishnah*, the oral interpretations of Torah. This was a critical next step in Jewish education. If Bet Sefer taught what the Scriptures said, Bet Talmud taught what those Scriptures meant and how to live them out.

Jewish people believed that the Mishnah had been handed down to Joshua by Moses, just like the written Torah. It was passed down orally from one person to another, from generation to generation, prohibited from being written down. So, once again, this level of Jewish education was rooted in memorization, requiring the student to commit a host of Scriptures and teachings to memory.

For most of the young men who had made it this far, here is where their education ended. At the completion of Bet Talmud, they would go home, learn the family business, and continue to exercise their faith in their local synagogue and other settings. But if they showed real promise, if they were among the best of the best, they would be invited to enter the highest form of Jewish education: *Bet Midrash*.

In Bet Midrash (pronounced *bayt mee-drahsh*), students focused not only on the written and oral torahs but also on how rabbis, past and present, had interpreted these teachings. Expectations were extremely high. Students were required to memorize much of the Scripture and traditions and to be able to share a specific rabbi's interpretation on command. In many ways, they were being entrusted with the memory of the faith, preparing to pass it down to future generations.

So, if at the end of Bet Midrash a student continued to show exceptional promise, he would take the final step in his education: he would seek out a rabbi in hopes of becoming his disciple. His goal would be to follow that rabbi wherever he went, studying and memorizing his every teaching, observing his every action, hoping not only to learn everything that his rabbi knew, but more important, to become like his rabbi in every way.

To follow a rabbi, though, a disciple could not simply make a request. He had to be invited. He would pursue that rabbi, working hard to convince him that he had what it took, that he could carry the yoke of that rabbi. And if the rabbi finally decided to take him on as a disciple, the young man would hear this rabbi say two words:

"*Lech acharai*" (lech akh-a-rye).

Follow me.

> A rabbi's "yoke" was his unique interpretation of Scripture and expectations of his disciples.

When Jesus speaks these words, Simon knows exactly what they mean: Jesus is offering him the opportunity to become his disciple. But this means that to accept this offer, Simon, just like any other disciple, will have to sacrifice greatly. He will have to leave behind his wife, his job, his home, everything that is familiar, to go wherever Jesus goes and do whatever Jesus commands him to do.

> The men Jesus calls to be his disciples are not exceptional. They aren't unique. They are people just like you and me. They all washed out of rabbi school and had to go learn a trade. What sets them apart is that, when asked to follow Jesus, knowing full well what it would cost them, they said yes.

There's another layer to look at. The fact that Jesus is inviting Simon to be his disciple while Simon is working as a fisherman means that Simon isn't currently following another rabbi. At some point, whether in Bet Sefer or Bet Talmud, he was told, "You aren't good enough. Go learn your family trade."

In selecting Simon, Jesus shows that he isn't gathering his disciples from among the best and most promising students. Quite the opposite. He is choosing students whom other rabbis rejected.

For much of my life, I elevated the disciples to a status high above those of us living today. These were the men who literally followed

Jesus. Clearly, they must be holier and more righteous than the rest of us.

But in this moment, we see that the men Jesus calls to be his disciples are not exceptional. They aren't unique. They are people just like you and me. They all washed out of rabbi school and had to go learn a trade.

What sets them apart is that, when asked to follow Jesus, knowing full well what it would cost them, they said yes.

Will we?

Jesus is still inviting people to be his disciples. And just as it was back then, this is an invitation that comes at a cost, an offer that asks for our full devotion and complete surrender. Jesus is asking us to commit our entire lives to him, to make him our Lord and Savior, to follow him wherever he leads, and to trust him no matter what he asks.

We are the fish that Jesus is longing to catch. And yet, while in this parable we are the ones getting caught in the net, sacrificing everything to follow Jesus, what Jesus will reveal is that, in the end, he will be "caught" and sacrificed on our behalf so that through him we might truly live.

Episode 5

CUPS

Now John's disciples and the Pharisees were fasting. Some people came and asked Jesus, "How is it that John's disciples and the disciples of the Pharisees are fasting, but yours are not?" Jesus answered, "How can the guests of the bridegroom fast while he is with them? They cannot, so long as they have him with them. But the time will come when the bridegroom will be taken from them, and on that day they will fast."

(Mark 2:18–20 NIV)

The response Jesus gave when asked why his disciples didn't fast may feel strange to us, even random. He gave what appeared to be a cryptic analogy about bridegrooms being taken away from their guests.

To his Jewish audience, however, these images would have made a very clear point: weddings are meant for celebration. Just as wedding guests would never fast during the festivities, people should not fast while the Messiah is here. This was a time to rejoice!

Jesus used this analogy because he knew it was something all Jews could relate to. Everyone in his audience had attended a wedding before. It was an event that involved the entire community.

But as we see in episode 5, when Jesus attends a wedding in Cana, not all weddings are joy-filled. Sometimes celebrations mask tension and strife. For the family of the groom, this is a day of unparalleled stress. And in this scene, everything seems to be going wrong!

Fortunately, Jesus is there to fix it. Soon, cups will be filled and celebrations can resume.

But in the midst of all this, we realize that Jesus has his own cup to drink from, his own fears and worries that lurk beneath the surface. What allows him to relieve the suffering of others is actually the very thing that causes him to suffer. And by the end of this wedding, some will not only begin to understand what that is but also to see how it promises a far greater celebration than they have ever experienced, one that will extend far beyond this small village—perhaps even to the ends of the earth.

Chapter 17

FAMILY MATTERS

One day, when my wife was a child, she went shopping with her parents. Like any child, she quickly became bored and searched for ways to entertain herself. As she looked at the many circular racks of clothing around the store, she had an idea: Wouldn't it be fun to hide inside them? At that age, she was so small that she could completely conceal herself, even as people searched through the clothes on the rack.

So, she made a game of it.

After a few minutes, her parents realized she was gone. For what seemed to them like ages, they searched the entire store, calling her name, scouring through every rack, finding no trace of their daughter.

Finally, when they had begun to assume the absolute worst, their little daughter jumped out and shouted, "Surprise!"

They were not amused.

There are few things more terrifying to a parent than losing a child. Your heart races. You can hardly breathe. Seconds feel like hours, and with each passing moment, your mind drifts to ever darker places.

Imagine how much more terrifying it would be to lose a child in a major city, surrounded by hundreds of thousands of people—especially when that child is the Son of God!

As episode 5 begins, Jesus' parents are living this nightmare. The Passover festival has concluded and thousands of people are in the city, but Jesus is nowhere to be found.

This scene is a depiction of the events described in Luke 2, when a twelve-year-old Jesus and his family visited the Jerusalem temple.

> And after the days were completed, while they were returning, the boy Jesus stayed behind in Jerusalem. And his parents did not know it, but believing him to be in the group of travelers, they went a day's journey. And they began searching for him among their relatives and their acquaintances, and when they did not find him, they returned to Jerusalem to search for him. (vv. 43–45)

Luke tells us that it took Mary and Joseph three days to find Jesus.

Can you imagine that? Three days with no idea where your child is? Three days hoping you will find him safe and alive in a city that, because of the Passover celebration, is filled beyond capacity with people from all over the world?

It makes you wonder: How could Mary and Joseph lose sight of Jesus? How do you misplace the Son of God? To those of us living thousands of years later, this seems unfathomable. But to those living at the time of Jesus, it was quite plausible.

You see, Jesus came from the small village of Nazareth. At that time, its population was only around one hundred to four hundred people, many of whom were related to one another. So, Jesus grew up surrounded by his extended family.

When a festival like Passover occurred, every able-bodied person in the village would travel to Jerusalem in a large caravan. Passover was one of three Jewish holy days when God's people were required to physically worship in the temple. Jesus would have made this trip alongside his aunts, uncles, cousins, and other neighbors from Nazareth.

He also would have returned with them.

So, as Mary and Joseph began the trip back home from Jerusalem, they assumed that Jesus was with other members of their family. They had made this journey three times a year for the past twelve years or so. This likely wasn't the first time they were in a situation like this. Caravans could become crowded and spread apart. As far as they knew, Jesus was simply in a part of the caravan that they couldn't see and would rejoin them at camp in the evening.

Mary says something to this effect in the episode. She tells Jesus, "You were supposed to be in the caravan with Uncle Abijah!" Mary's family was likely so large and close that it was natural for her to assume that others were looking out for Jesus. She knew they would guard and protect him at any cost.

As we read further into the Gospels, though, we get the sense that these family bonds began to strain over time. While Mary and Joseph's love for Jesus never changed, his relationships with his other family members seemed to grow more tense.

Mark's gospel gives an awkward account of an interaction between Jesus and his family early on in his ministry.

> Then Jesus entered a house, and again a crowd gath-
> ered, so that he and his disciples were not even able
> to eat. When his family heard about this, they went

to take charge of him, for they said, *"He is out of his mind."* ...

Then Jesus' mother and brothers arrived. Standing outside, they sent someone in to call him. A crowd was sitting around him, and they told him, "Your mother and brothers are outside looking for you."

"Who are my mother and my brothers?" he asked. (3:20–21, 31–33 NIV, emphasis added)

The tension in these verses is palpable. And yet, Mark isn't the only gospel to record such family drama. John tells us that "even his brothers didn't believe in him" (John 7:5 NLT).

It is hard to imagine how Jesus' own family members could doubt him. Did they not notice that there was something different about him as he grew up? Had Mary and Joseph not told them about the messages from the angels?

But before we judge the situation too quickly, consider the circumstances they and other Jews were facing at that time and what exactly it was about Jesus that his family members were opposing: The Jewish people were in the grip of the Roman Empire. They had been conquered and oppressed for generations. Many people were longing for the Messiah to arrive and be the warrior king who would break off the shackles of Rome and liberate the people once again.

As far as Jesus' family could tell, Jesus was no warrior. Nor was he claiming to be. His message seemed to have nothing to do with overthrowing Roman governors or taking back the land.

Even if that were his message, though, they still may have been hesitant to support him. Such claims would have presented another problem. Rome did not permit sedition or rebellion. If they sensed that Jesus was going to form a violent uprising, they would not only have executed him but would also have eliminated anyone they considered to be his accomplices—including his family.

The people of Nazareth had watched this happen in Sepphoris, a neighboring village fewer than four miles away. They knew it could happen to them as well.

So, in the end, Jesus' family had many reasons not to believe in him. Whether it was out of fear or out of doubt, they determined that life would be better if Jesus simply stopped making such bold claims about himself.

> There is no amount of suffering that God will not endure to reach us.

And yet, while this may have been desirable to them, it could have been devastating to Jesus. How do you handle the rejection of those you love? What must it feel like to be abandoned by those who had nurtured and raised you?

In many ways, though, this rejection was part of Jesus' cup of suffering. Jesus would suffer loss after loss, rejection after rejection, abuse after abuse—so much so that his death on the cross would be but his final act of suffering. He would lose all that he loved to demonstrate the depths of his love for us.

In those moments when we feel rejected in our lives, when we are separated from those we love, we must remember these Scriptures that show us that Jesus has been there too. He is proof that God knows our suffering and that God cares. There is no amount of suffering that God will not endure to reach us. This is how much you matter to God.

As episode 5 continues, Jesus makes it clear that we have only just begun to explore the depths of that love and to see the effect that it will have on us and everything around us.

Chapter 18

BIBLE STUDIES AND ELECTRIC SLIDES

It is hard to imagine Jesus partying, isn't it? In most artistic depictions, Jesus looks so somber and serious. He is on a mission and will not be deterred; he has no room for fun and games.

These depictions, however, do not reflect a Jewish Jesus, because the Jews of Jesus' day had no problem throwing a party. They did so often and well—especially when it came to weddings!

Weddings were an opportunity for celebration, a reminder of the union between God and Israel. The *chuppa* (pronounced *khoop-paw*), or wedding arch, was an illustration of how the Hebrew people stood beneath Mount Sinai as they entered into a covenant relationship with God. The *ketubah* (pronounced *keh-too-baw*), or wedding contract, was a reflection of the Ten Commandments, which may be seen as the Israelites' marriage covenant with God. These and other symbols reminded the community of who they were and who God was continuing to call them to be.

Wine was served to mark the celebration. People prayed the kiddush, just as they did on Shabbat and at festivals, thanking God for their abundance. It was even common to fill cups with wine to the brim so that they "runneth over," testifying to God's overflowing blessings.[1]

But there was also another element of these wedding celebrations that would surprise us and probably feel rather strange and awkward at our modern weddings: Bible study.

> Tachat תחת, which is translated "at the foot of [Mount Sinai]," describes the lowest regions of a place. It is often used to describe Sheol, the place of the dead, which existed "beneath" the earth. This gives the suggestion that the Hebrew people are standing "beneath" Mount Sinai.

There is a moment in episode 5 when Jesus is sitting at a table, using cups to demonstrate something to a group of children. It could be that he is playing a game simply to entertain them. But it is also just as likely that he is instructing them in the Torah.

At the time of Jesus, as we've seen, people took every opportunity to teach Scripture. It wasn't restricted to Bet Midrash or synagogue gatherings; it didn't even require a religious teacher to be present. The sounds of people discussing the Torah were common throughout towns and villages.

It was common to discuss the Torah at weddings or other special gatherings. There is even a saying in the Mishnah: "When three eat at one table and the words of the Torah are not spoken there, it is as if they ate at the altars of the dead ... but when three eat at one table and bring up the words of the Torah, it is as if they ate from the table of God" (*Mishnah*, Avot 3:4).[2]

Can you imagine if this were still commonplace today? What if, at the wedding reception, somewhere between the cutting of the cake and the electric slide (a dance), a pastor came over and began to lead a Bible study at your table?

Perhaps you might go along with it, not wanting to be rude. But it would feel strange, wouldn't it? It just isn't normal.

How did this happen? Why does the idea of a mid-reception Bible study feel like a recipe for disaster? When did our lives become separated into "regular life" and "spiritual life"—as if those are two entirely different things?

At the time of Jesus, this was unfathomable. People could not imagine their relationship with God being disconnected from any part of their lives; the two were completely integrated.

This is going to be very important for Jesus. Because as the wedding progresses, problems are going to arise—problems that only Jesus can solve. But for Jesus, this won't simply be an opportunity to perform a miracle. This will be an opportunity to teach, to reveal something very important about himself, and to remind those in attendance of a Scripture that explains everything.

And he needs for them to be ready to hear it.

Chapter 19

A JOURNEY WITH NO MAP

On my first trip to the Holy Land, we spent the beginning of the week in the Negev desert, which in Scripture is often called the *wilderness* (e.g., Gen. 21:21). It was the beginning of July, and both the sun and the heat were intense.

What made the trip more challenging was that, rather than traveling throughout the country by bus, we were hiking eight to ten miles per day. I'll admit I was nervous about this at first. Hiking in the desert in the heat of the summer seemed daunting, perhaps even dangerous.

But as the days progressed, I realized I was experiencing something unique and beautiful, something few people ever do. I wasn't just seeing Israel—I was also smelling, hearing, and basking in this land that God's people had protected and cherished for generations. Rather than rushing from site to site, I had time to savor each step, imagining myself walking the same paths with those who had traversed this land long ago.

One day in the wilderness, our guide did something that allowed us to experience this in an especially powerful way. Soon after we set off on our hike, he started walking in a circular route. He began at one spot, hiked over rocks and through ditches, and eventually returned to where he had started.

For the first several rounds of this, we followed our guide in a loose line, talking with one another and taking in the landscape. But as time wore on, we realized he was trying to teach us something.

Each time we walked this route, we noticed the little things he was doing. For instance, he would always step on a certain stone or pick up a rock and toss it in a specific direction. He did this over and over, until eventually it became clear that he wanted us to imitate him.

We didn't realize it at the time, but our guide was giving us a powerful glimpse into the life of a disciple. He was showing us what it was like to "follow" Jesus.

During the wedding celebration in episode 5, we listen as several of Jesus' disciples gather around a table and discuss what life will be like with their new rabbi. Simon comments that though the custom was for a disciple to choose his rabbi, that wasn't the case for them. Instead, Jesus had chosen them. This is an honor they never expected. But they also realize that it is a commitment that may cost them everything.

Today, when we hear the word *disciple* in a Christian context, we assume it means someone who believes in Jesus and tries to live according to the Bible. And while these aspects of the relationship are true, they don't convey the intense nature of discipleship in the first century.

As I've mentioned, a man who became a disciple would leave everything behind to follow his rabbi. He would journey for months at a time away from his wife, his kids, his home, and his job to go where his rabbi went and do what his rabbi instructed. His mission was not simply to learn everything his rabbi knew but to try to become his rabbi.

Just as I did that day in the Negev, a disciple would follow in his rabbi's footsteps exactly. If his rabbi stopped, he would stop. If his rabbi picked up a stone, he would too. A disciple saw his rabbi's every action as an opportunity to learn.

In fact, it was believed that a rabbi's smallest behaviors were some of his most important. Disciples would watch how their rabbi ate, how he prayed, how he untied his sandals. No act was insignificant. They believed that they honored their rabbi through imitation and obedience.

Throughout the Gospels, we catch glimpses of this relationship. Jesus often taught in parables, expecting his disciples to observe his behavior and listen for answers. The disciples asked Jesus questions, hoping to gain his unique perspective. And over time, we see the disciples evolve from mere students to practitioners. Jesus even sent them out on their own to apply what they had learned (see Mark 6:7–12).

This is what it looks like to be a disciple of Jesus.

As the disciples sit around the table at the wedding, discussing the life that awaits them, they feel both excited and unworthy. In many ways, it is a cup from which they must drink, a burden they must bear. Just as Jesus carries the weight of his suffering with him throughout his ministry, his disciples will carry the weight of their responsibility.

In the end, Jesus would look upon each of them and command them to "go and make disciples of all nations, baptizing them in the name of the Father and of the Son and of the Holy Spirit, and teaching them to obey everything I have commanded you" (Matt. 28:19–20a NIV). This would be his Great Commission to them, the culmination of all that he had taught them. They would be his reflection in the world, and they would disciple others to do the same.

How would you feel if you were sitting around the table with Jesus' disciples in this episode? What would be your response to the cup that awaits you, this awesome honor and responsibility that Jesus has given you?

In a sense, we do sit beside these disciples at that table. The Great Commission is our responsibility. The cup they must drink from is also the one we must drink from.

As the episode concludes, Jesus' disciples will get a taste of exactly where that responsibility will lead. For, as he performs his first public miracle, Jesus will actually reveal both who he is and what he has come to do.

Chapter 20

MORE THAN JUST A MIRACLE

I had a big wedding. Since my wife grew up in the church where we got married and I was one of the pastors, we invited the entire church to attend. Hundreds of people came. Afterward, the congregation threw us a reception. And later that evening, we had a small, private, family reception. From start to finish, our wedding and receptions lasted more than ten hours. That seemed like a lot!

If we had lived at the time of Jesus, though, our wedding would have just been getting started.

Throughout episode 5, we see only a small portion of the wedding of Asher and Sarah. Typically, first-century Jewish wedding celebrations lasted an entire week. A Jewish wedding was a social event to which friends, family, and members of the community were all invited.

The celebration began with the groom carrying his bride from her parents' home to his parents' home. He would be surrounded by friends who would dance as they processed through the streets. Those they passed would light lamps and join them for the rest of the journey.[1]

Once the bride and groom arrived home, the real festivities would begin. Attendees would toast the bride and groom, there would be songs and dancing, and there would be an abundance of food.

It was expected of the family to provide enough wine and food to satisfy all the guests throughout the weeklong celebration. Failure to do so would result in great shame upon the family.

These expectations set the stage for us to understand the problems that arose at the wedding at Cana. Not long after the celebration has started, Mary came to Jesus, informing him that the wine had run out.

This is concerning on two levels. First, since wine is used throughout Judaism as a mark of celebration, allowing the wine to run out would suggest that the celebration has ended prematurely. Second, as we've seen, this unfortunate circumstance would bring great shame upon the family. Guests would assume that the hosts had either planned poorly or could not afford enough wine for the entire celebration. Either way, much was at stake.

In the episode, Mary approaches her Son, asking him to set things right. At first, Jesus demurs, saying that his time has not come. But Mary ignores his objections and directs the servants to follow his instructions, whatever they might be. Jesus decides not only to grant Mary's request but also to use this moment to reveal his glory to those in attendance.

John's gospel tells us that "six stone water jars were set there, in accordance with the ceremonial cleansing of the Jews, each holding two or three measures. Jesus said to them, 'Fill the water jars with water.' And they filled them to the brim" (2:6–7).

The fact that John tells us that there were six *stone* jars is no mere detail. There is a reason Jesus selects these specific vessels rather than some other container for his miracle.

Remember, weddings were an opportunity for scriptural teaching. So, as Jesus performs this miracle, he is taking advantage of his audience's openness to God's Word. If anyone saw that Jesus had done this miracle with water from stone jars intended for ritual purification, the Scriptures they had memorized as children—that they discussed every week on Shabbat and may have even studied at this wedding—would have come to mind. They would have remembered Ezekiel 36, where God says, "I will sprinkle on you pure water, and you will be clean from all of your uncleanness, and I will cleanse you from all of your idols. And I will give a new heart to you, and a new spirit I will give into your inner parts, and I will remove the heart of stone from your flesh, and I will give to you a heart of flesh" (vv. 25–26).

And they would have realized that Jesus wasn't there just to save a wedding feast.

Those verses from Ezekiel are situated within a long passage in which God both recalls Israel's past shame and offers them hope for the future. They have turned their backs on the Lord and pursued other gods. God promises not only to redeem them from their circumstances but also to redeem their hearts.

Those attending the wedding know that the Israelites' situation in Ezekiel was not that much different from their own. God's people are suffering. They have been unfaithful. They need to be redeemed.

By using these stone jars intended for ritual purification, Jesus is signaling that he is here to do the same thing God promised in Ezekiel. He is here to transform the hearts of God's people. He is here to restore and redeem them.

People who knew Jesus may have doubted what kind of Messiah he was, or if he even was the Messiah. But in this moment, Jesus makes everything clear. He is indeed the Messiah, and he wields the power of God.

As the servants draw wine from the jars and pour them into the cups of those in attendance, this message is not lost on his first followers. John says that by doing this miracle, Jesus "revealed his glory, and his disciples believed in him" (John 2:11). Whatever doubts they might have had, whatever questions lingered, it became clear that they were not following a typical rabbi. The cups they now hold in their hands are but a foreshadowing of the cup they will one day drink from. Both sweet and bitter, it is far greater than they ever could have imagined.

Episode 6

ACCEPTANCE

There are few things more important in our lives than acceptance. Sometimes we don't even realize this. Perhaps we don't think we need it. But as human beings, we thrive on acceptance.

As children, we bring art projects home to our parents, longing for their approval and acceptance of our talents.

As teenagers, we seek out social groups, yearning for even a small gathering who will embrace us as one of their own.

And as we progress through adulthood, we long for our lives to matter. We yearn for significance, hoping others will accept and appreciate who we are and what we have to offer.

We don't have to be universally accepted—we just need confirmation that someone out there agrees with us, embraces us, and values us.

This becomes even more clear to us when we consider it from the opposite perspective. Can you imagine not being accepted? Can you imagine if there was no one who valued you? Who agreed with you? Who welcomed you?

Jesus was not an attention seeker. In fact, Jesus often went to great lengths to avoid celebrity and to remove himself from crowds. Nevertheless, he understood the importance of acceptance.

This is especially apparent in episode 6, when Jesus encounters several people who have been rejected by society. They are not welcome, not wanted, not accepted. Jesus will change this.

The question that should burden us as we watch is: While Jesus enables others to be accepted, will we truly accept him?

Chapter 21

HOW TO CONQUER A PEOPLE

It is amazing how quickly memory fades. Something can be the most important thought on our minds at one moment and completely forgotten soon afterward. The most popular celebrity of our childhood is possibly someone our children have never heard of. That historical event that consumed our thoughts for years may eventually become little more than a memorial date on our calendars.

That argument that once seemed so important is now something we can hardly remember.

The reality is that time can seem to move quickly. People and events can be recorded, but the feelings and experiences of past generations are much more difficult to capture. Many of them are quickly and easily forgotten, even within a generation. Culture changes. Language evolves. And old ways of doing things may come to seem strange and foreign to those who come after.

To us, who live almost two thousand years removed from the events of the Gospels, it is nearly impossible to imagine what it was like to live in the Roman Empire of Jesus' day. Books can tell us of the people who lived, the battles they fought, the customs they practiced, and the languages they spoke, but they can scarcely help us imagine the reality of living in that world day after day.

The people living at the time of Jesus, however, could imagine it quite well. They were surrounded by Rome and its influence. The roads they traveled, the items they purchased, and the laws they obeyed all reflected the growing power and impact of the empire.

> Part of what is behind their desire for this grand empire of happy Roman citizens is that when citizens embrace Roman ideals, they don't revolt. Revolts are costly and chaotic, and Rome hates chaos. They want order in the empire.

From the very first episode, *The Chosen* attempts to bring us into this world. The praetor, Quintus, is a vessel of Rome's power and control. The centurion, Gaius, is its enforcer. And in episode 6, there is a line of dialogue that reflects clearly what it was like to live within the grip of this occupying military force.

Quintus wants to impress a childhood rival who is traveling to Capernaum, so he looks to Matthew for advice. In this fictional exchange, Matthew responds that Quintus should share with his rival his plans for infrastructure, explaining that "conquest is not simply conquering nations but imposing a way of life."

With this statement, Matthew, a Jewish man, summarizes Rome's approach to imperialism. As the empire expanded throughout the world, Rome's goal was not simply to obtain more land and defeat more people. Their goal was to spread the glory of Rome. They wanted the entire world to be Roman, to embrace the Roman way of life, and to identify themselves as part of this grand civilization.

Men like Quintus and Gaius exist to accomplish this aim. Their purpose is to foster acceptance for the Roman Empire within their region of responsibility. They might not be able to force people to love Rome, but they can force the people to obey, and they can encourage them to assimilate.

As praetor, Quintus is primarily an administrator. His main responsibility is to maintain order in his region. He commands an army and wields considerable power, but he is also bound by bureaucracy. His personal goal is to rise to a higher position, and the best way he can do this is to compel his populace to accept Roman authority.

In a rebellious region such as Galilee, though, this is no easy task. So Quintus relies on soldiers like Gaius to execute his objectives. As a centurion, Gaius was responsible for a centuria, a group of about eighty soldiers.[1] These men would be used to build infrastructure, fight military engagements, and promote the general peace.

> "The rank designated for the commander of a Roman centuria, a subdivision of a cohort. At full strength the centuria would constitute 80 soldiers (not the hundred that the name implies)." — Dennis M. Swanson

In many areas of the empire, these basic forces would have been enough to maintain order. Quintus would have had little trouble being successful in his role. But this was Israel, and Israel would not surrender easily.

Not only had Israel been subjected to one conquering nation after another for centuries, but the Roman way of life directly conflicted with the commands of the Torah. The Jewish people would not worship the gods of the Roman pantheon or acknowledge the emperor as divine. They refused to break the Sabbath, defile their temple, or embrace the immoralities of Roman art and culture.

Rome had entered their land with promises of salvation, declarations that all would be well now that they were in power. But the Jewish people were seeking fulfillment of those promises elsewhere. They were looking for the biblical Messiah.

Just like people today, the people of the first century lived in a world where they were surrounded by voices shouting, "Choose me! I am the one who can rescue you. Let me be your savior." Today, these voices call out through commercials, social media, politicians, and influencers. Perhaps some are coming to your mind right now.

God's people have always been faced with the difficult task of choosing whether to look to the Lord or look to other sources as their Savior. In Old Testament days, the temptation was to rely on the pagan gods of surrounding nations. Today, it is products and personalities that we are tempted to put our faith in. And at the time of Jesus, it was Rome and its vast empire that people were coaxed to trust.

The question, though, doesn't seem to be whether the Jewish people will choose someone other than God's promised Messiah. Rather, it is whether they will recognize and accept him once he arrives.

Chapter 22

STAY ONE HUNDRED CUBITS AWAY

As I mentioned, when I visited Israel, the first leg of our trip took us through the Negev. We went to the Dead Sea, Earth's lowest elevation on land, over 1,300 feet below sea level. It derives its name from its salt content, which is an unbelievable 34 percent, a salinity that prevents all forms of life except bacteria.

I can only imagine what it must have been like for those who discovered this magnificent body of water. After a lengthy journey through the desert, they stumbled upon what appeared to be an oasis, enough water to sustain them forever, only to find that not only is it salty, it's lethal.

Nevertheless, while the Dead Sea might not be potable, it is rich in other ways. In fact, since long before the time of Jesus, people would travel to the Dead Sea for its reputed healing qualities. Rashes, infections, and other skin conditions would seem to disappear after bathing in these waters.

It is no surprise, then, that the man with leprosy in episode 6 says that he is selling his tools before making his way to the Dead Sea. He is hoping that the stories are true and that this will be the journey that finally frees him of his burden.

The term *leprosy* can actually refer to a variety of skin conditions outlined in Leviticus 10. It can be anything from eczema to Hansen's disease, which is what most people think of when they hear the word *leprosy* today.[1] But what made leprosy such an awful condition wasn't simply the skin disease itself; it was the social consequences.

When people contracted one of these skin conditions, they were considered ritually unclean. This meant that for a period of time they would have to be isolated from the rest of the community.

But what happens if the condition never goes away? Worse, what happens when that condition is contagious?

To have leprosy was to be completely unaccepted by society. In fact, soon after the time of Jesus, rules were established that forbade a person from being within four cubits (about six feet) of someone with leprosy if the one with disease were downwind, and one hundred cubits (one hundred and fifty feet) if they were upwind. Not only was the leper considered to be unclean himself, but also he posed a threat to everyone around him.

Can you imagine the surprise and concern among the disciples, then, when Jesus approaches a man with leprosy? In the episode, the disciples are terrified and angry. John threatens violence against the man. He could make their rabbi unclean, possibly removing him from their lives permanently.

And yet, while no one else might accept this man, Jesus does: "A man with leprosy came and knelt before him and said, 'Lord, if you are willing, you can make me clean.' Jesus reached out his hand and touched the man. 'I am willing,' he said. 'Be clean!' Immediately he was cleansed of his leprosy (Matt. 8:2–3 NIV).

Jesus doesn't just *see* this man. He doesn't just listen to him. He does what no one else will do: He touches him. He accepts him and thus makes him acceptable.

This man's condition was something no one could cure. Rome might promise salvation to those who accept their empire, but nothing they offered could free this man from the stigma of his disease. The religious leaders stood ready to accept him if he could be healed, but there was nothing they could do to make that healing happen.

Jesus, however, does both. He heals him of his disease and his stigma. And in doing so, he shows us what true healing looks like.

By touching this man, Jesus reminds him of who he is in the eyes of God. He is more than his disease, more than the circumstances of his life. He is loved and he has value. And once the man is free of this disease, he can finally experience being accepted by his community again.

From this moment forward, this man's identity will forever be tied to Jesus. His past will no longer define him. Instead, his life will be defined by who Jesus has allowed him to be.

This is no small thing. For, at the time of Jesus, people deeply believed that a person's past had a direct impact on their present and possibly even their future. They believed that the stories and actions of your ancestors directly reflected on you and how people perceived you.

So, as the episode progresses, the focus shifts. Jesus has just freed this man from the trauma of his past. The question is: Can Jesus escape the perceived blemishes on his own past? And will this be a barrier that will ultimately keep people from accepting him?

Chapter 23

WHO IS YOUR DADDY AND WHAT DID HE DO?

Have you ever researched your ancestry? Perhaps you completed one of those DNA tests that trace your genetic origins. Or maybe you looked through old photos and birth certificates, re-creating your family tree.

It is amazing what we learn when we discover who our ancestors were. When I looked into my own genealogy, I found that I could trace my roots to some of the earliest American settlers. I learned that my relatives were present at major events in history. I even discovered that I am distantly related to several celebrities.

I also uncovered some unsavory relations. I found that I have ancestors who were wanted by the law and others who were responsible for ruining the lives of entire families. They are humbling reminders of imperfection.

And yet, they are part of my story. For better or worse, they had a hand in the events that led to my life. Had they made different decisions or stumbled onto different paths, my own story would almost certainly be different.

I think we all realize this to some degree or another. We innately understand that our ancestry shapes us. We are the product of our predecessors. This was certainly the belief at the time of Jesus.

There is a moment in episode 6 when Jesus is sitting in the home of Zebedee and Salome, the parents of John and Big James. This appears to be one of the first times that Zebedee and Salome have been able to sit down and interview this man they believe to be the Messiah, a man their sons left everything to follow. Zebedee asks Jesus, "What was your father's lineage?"

Today, this might seem like a very strange question to ask. When we read the Bible, many of us skip over the lists of how so-and-so begat the son of so-and-so, who begat so-and-so, for generation after generation. But at the time of Jesus, a genealogy served as one's introduction. In Western society, we introduce ourselves with our names, where we live, and our occupations. These are things that we believe define us and have value in our society. At the time of Jesus, though, it was one's ancestors who served this purpose.

The Jews believed that a person was a reflection of his or her family's personality and values. If a man was honest, for example, people would automatically assume that his sons and grandsons would be honest. At the same time, if they had been dishonest, people would assume the worst.

These assumptions spanned generations. The Hebrew word *ben*, which means "son," could refer to one's direct descendant or even someone generations later. So, in the eyes of the Jewish community, a person's genealogy could explain the greatness from which he descended, the shame from which he was running, or a variety of other characteristics.

When Zebedee asks Jesus about his lineage, he is looking to make an assessment of Jesus. *Does this man come from a good line? Should my sons be following him? Is his family worthy of his claim that he is the Messiah?*

It is this last question that makes Jesus' response so interesting. In the show, the screenwriters imagine Jesus answering that he descends from "Josiah, father of Jechoniah at the time of the exile." This is a response designed to evoke mixed reactions.

On the one hand, the two men that Jesus mentions are both kings. And since it was commonly believed that the Messiah would be a king who would reclaim the throne of Israel, Jesus' answer would establish his connection to the royal line of King David. At the same time, however, Jesus is referencing one of the bleakest moments in his family's history, and one of the worst kings with whom to be associated.

Matthew mentions King Jechoniah in his gospel's genealogy of Jesus: "Josiah became the father of Jechoniah and his brothers, at the time of the deportation to Babylon. And after the deportation to Babylon, Jechoniah became the father of Shealtiel" (Matt. 1:11–12).

When we examine this lineage more closely, we discover that Jechoniah isn't actually the son of Josiah—at least not in the way we think of it. This is an instance in which words such as *father* and *son* are used to refer to people in a family line who are generations apart. Jechoniah (who also goes by the name *Jehoiachin*) is actually the son of King Jehoiakim. Both of these men were kings during the events leading up to the Babylonian exile. In many ways, they were responsible for this terrible part of Israel's history!

So, by referencing this particular part of Jesus' ancestry, Matthew and *The Chosen* are intentionally linking Jesus to these men. At first glance, this seems like a strange decision. Of all the people in Jesus' lineage, why highlight these men? How is this shameful connection supposed to reflect well upon Jesus?

But the reality is that this connection to Jechoniah is significant not because it highlights similarities between him and Jesus but because it reveals how they are different.

Jesus and Jechoniah are both kings, yes. But they are very different kinds of kings. Jechoniah was weak and unfaithful. He led the people into bondage. Jesus, however, will be a good King, a true King, one who will set God's people free. He will be the opposite of who Jechoniah was.

For many, the blemishes on Jesus' lineage may be enough reason to reject him, to write him off as a false Messiah. But for those who are willing to accept him, they, like the man with leprosy, will experience how Jesus overcomes our past. He will prove that we are not bound by the mistakes we or those who came before us have made. Through him, we can have new life, a new story, and the freedom to write a new chapter, with him as the central figure.

Chapter 24

WILL YOU ACCEPT THIS?

Acceptance is not always easy, is it? We can know that something is true, but our minds may still have a difficult time accepting it.

For instance, imagine that you've gone to the hospital to visit someone who is very sick. Perhaps she has cancer that has spread throughout her body. So, as you pray for her, you ask God to remove the cancer—and it happens! Suddenly, she is cancer-free.

Of course, you would praise God for healing this person. But would there also be part of you that finds this hard to accept? Had it really been God? Was my prayer really answered? Or is there another explanation?

Jesus faced this throughout his ministry. Often, he would try to quiet the excitement surrounding his miracles, knowing that this alone was not a solid foundation for faith in him. No matter what people saw or heard, if they had decided to reject him as Messiah, they could always find reasons to support their choice. Some might say his lineage wasn't good enough, that he didn't follow the law closely enough, or that he associated too much with sinful and diseased people. People might even argue that a poor, simple rabbi like Jesus could never provide the salvation people needed, not in the ways that a mighty empire like Rome could.

So, as Jesus sits in the home of Zebedee and Salome, teaching the crowd that has formed, he is aware that these questions linger in the minds of those present. And he recognizes that the people around him are at varying stages of belief. Some may accept him and truly believe he can save them; others doubt the miracles taking place right in front of them.

On the faithful side, there are the friends of the paralyzed man. Unable to reach even the door to the house, they carry their friend to the roof, tearing away the layers of clay, brush, and beams to lower him down to Jesus. As they do this, they must certainly realize the trouble they are causing and the damage this inflicts on this family's home. But they are desperate. They believe Jesus can do what no other has been able to achieve.

Mark's gospel records it this way: "When they were not able to bring him to him because of the crowd, they removed the roof where he was. And after digging through, they lowered the stretcher on which the paralytic was lying. And when Jesus saw their faith, he said to the paralytic, 'Child, your sins are forgiven'" (2:4–5).

Jesus' words catch the crowd's attention for two reasons. First, Jesus bases his decision to help not on the paralyzed man's faith, but on the faith of this man's friends. Just as it was believed that a person's illness could be a consequence of the sins of their ancestors, Jesus implies that this man's healing will happen because of the faith of his friends.

But notice that at this point Jesus doesn't specifically mention healing. Instead, he says that the man's sins are forgiven. This is the second thing that would have stood out to the crowd.

Jews believed that passages such as Psalm 32:5 and Isaiah 43:25 were proof that only God can forgive sins. So, it appears that by forgiving this man's sins, Jesus is either claiming God's authority or is claiming to actually be God!

To make sure there is no confusion, Jesus makes another bold statement. He looks at the religious leaders standing nearby, men who demonstrate their contempt for Jesus' claims, and says, "'Why are you considering these things in your hearts? Which is easier to say to the paralytic, "Your sins are forgiven," or to say "Get up and pick up your stretcher and walk"? But so that you may know that the Son of Man has authority on earth to forgive sins,'—he said to the paralytic—'I say to you, get up, pick up your stretcher, and go to your home'" (Mark 2:8b–11).

By using the phrase *Son of Man*, Jesus is referencing a passage from the Old Testament book of Daniel:

> In my vision at night I looked, and there before me was one like a son of man, coming with the clouds of heaven. He approached the Ancient of Days and was led into his presence. He was given authority, glory and sovereign power; all nations and peoples of every language worshiped him. His dominion is an everlasting dominion that will not pass away, and his kingdom is one that will never be destroyed. (7:13–14 NIV)

At the time of Jesus, *Son of Man* was commonly understood to be a reference to the Messiah.[1] But there was also a growing sense that the Son of Man might be more than a mere man. People saw connections between this passage in Daniel and a passage in Isaiah, where Isaiah says, "See, the LORD rides on a swift cloud and is coming to Egypt" (19:1 NIV). Both the Lord and the Son of Man are seen riding on clouds, thus linking the Son of Man with God's divine nature.

So, when Jesus identifies himself as the Son of Man and claims that the Son of Man has the authority to forgive sins, people immediately understand the implication: Jesus is claiming to be God.

But before they can even begin to debate such a claim, Jesus shifts their focus. He asks whether it's easier to forgive sins or to tell a paralyzed man to get up and walk.

In essence, Jesus is placing before them the question that has been appearing throughout this episode: Are you willing to accept this?

And then he heals the paralyzed man. While his critics are still probably preparing to answer that it's easier to claim to forgive sins, which no one can immediately verify, than to claim to have the power to heal paralysis, which anyone can instantly verify, Jesus goes right ahead and does the impossible thing, and their own eyes are forced to verify it.

The evidence is right there in front of them. Jesus is doing what no one else can do—not doctors or Romans or religious leaders. He is showing them what true salvation looks like.

Nevertheless, he knows how doubt creeps in. He knows that even as people depart, they will wrestle with whether to accept what they have just seen. They will question who to believe: the Romans and their bold promises, the religious leaders and their skepticism, or Jesus and his miraculous works.

In many ways, they are wrestling with the same struggles we face today. Every day, we are surrounded by voices that try to challenge our faith. Commercials, television personalities, and politicians make the same promises Rome did, claiming that they alone can provide that which will truly save us and make us happy.

And then there is Jesus—ever constant, ever present—having proven his deity not simply through the healing of one man but through his death and resurrection, an ultimate act of love that made possible the salvation of all humanity.

The answer seems obvious. And yet we still struggle with the same questions as Jesus' original audience:

Am I willing to accept this?

Am I willing to believe that Jesus is who he says he is and that he will do what he says he will do?

Am I willing to trust his voice over all the other voices?

Because if we can answer yes, then Jesus promises us a salvation we can find nowhere else, one that can guarantee the hope of new life. This offer is always there. We just have to accept it.

Episode 7

LEAVING

The month of August is always filled with tears for families with kids of a certain age. Sidewalks are lined with cars and vans stuffed with furniture and boxes. Strangers greet one another, ready to spend the next year sharing close quarters. Parents embrace their children, balancing the desire to hold on with the need to let go. This is the season of college drop-offs, a time when parents and children part ways. From this moment on, life for these families will never be the same.

I remember the day my parents dropped me off at college. I was excited to meet my roommates and explore this new campus. I heard afterward that my mom cried the whole way home.

A few weeks later, though, things shifted. Suddenly I was homesick. I missed my family, my room, the convenience of always having someone to cook my meals and do my laundry. And yet, even though my parents and I were experiencing similar pain, we all knew that it was right.

Leaving is an important part of life. Whether it is attending camp for the summer, moving off to college, or even getting married, these moments mark important milestones in our lives. We are stepping away from the life we knew, a life that was familiar and comfortable, and we are embarking upon something new.

Episode 7 features several of these moments. As people realize who Jesus truly is, they become acutely aware of the implications this will have on their lives. His presence changes everything. To follow him, they will need to surrender the lives they've led and the comforts and familiarities they have cherished. They will need to trust that this is an important milestone in their lives and that the path before them offers something greater than what they leave behind.

For some, this will be an easy choice. They will immediately leave everything to follow Jesus.

Others will struggle with it in the depths of their soul. And as good as Jesus' offer is, they may never actually be able to accept it.

Chapter 25

TRAVELING PREACHERS

I grew up in church. Everyone in my family—grandparents, cousins, aunts, uncles, and others—attended the same church. We took up two whole pews! I can still remember the sound of their voices around me each Sunday, singing hymns, offering prayers, quietly discussing whether we wanted to go to Cracker Barrel or the bagel shop for lunch.

I also remember this time in my life as a season of regular transition in my church. I grew up in a United Methodist church, so every few years, we would receive a new pastor. This happened so frequently that, honestly, it would have felt strange for a pastor to stay more than a few years.

You see, the Methodist Church operates on what is called an "itinerant" system. Rather than selecting what church they want to serve, pastors are appointed to a congregation by a bishop. This has its roots in the early days of Methodism, when Americans were so spread out that pastors would have to travel great distances just to reach everyone. They would ride on horseback along a "circuit," starting churches and caring for the congregations along that route. This system allowed the gospel to spread quickly and broadly throughout early America.

So, when I imagine the lifestyle of Jesus and his disciples, I can't help but picture those early Methodist practices. Jesus was an itinerant rabbi. He would travel from town to town around Galilee, preaching in synagogues and healing the people of those communities (see Matt. 4:23). In fact, he even sent his disciples out to do this on their own at certain points (see Mark 6:7–13). And yet, while the itinerant lifestyle was certainly filled with exciting experiences and fulfilling work, it also required incredible sacrifice.

> "For the most part these teachers did not hail from wealthy or priestly classes, but from the ranks of ordinary folk. They could be blacksmiths, tailors, farmers, tanners, shoemakers, woodcutters, and of course, carpenters. Many of them worked seasonally, traveling and teaching in the months when they were free." — Ann Spangler and Lois Tverberg

There is a moment in episode 7 when John, one of Jesus' disciples, is concerned for their safety after Jesus has upset some religious leaders. He asks Jesus if this is what he wants, to have to roam about from place to place, never able to settle down. We sense the danger Jesus faces as opposition rises against him. Though Jesus does not fear for his own safety, knowing his appointed time, the episode portrays his reticence to linger too long among large crowds.

Jesus' ministry, however, would have been mobile even if it had not been for these dangers. An itinerant rabbi and his disciples would travel for several months out of the year.[1] They would leave their families behind, entrusting their care and protection to others. They relied on this charity, never charging for their work.[2]

It was a life of simplicity and instability. And to the people of the first century, it was normal.

Perhaps what ought to strike us as most amazing is that Jesus chose this lifestyle. God put on flesh, but rather than claiming an earthly throne or surrounding himself with possessions and wealth, Jesus chose a life of wandering and sleeping on the ground, a life where it would have been normal for him to remain unmarried, a life where he would carry few possessions and have limited influence. He chose to be a common man among common people.

In other words, Jesus was willing to leave behind the splendor of heaven, the power of his throne, and the worship and praise of the heavenly host to walk the earth as a poor, itinerant preacher who would be reviled as often as he was revered.

This is the depth of God's love for us. There is no limit to what God would do to reach us. God proved that he is willing to humiliate himself to be with us and draw us back into relationship with him.

This kind of love is what Jesus illustrated through the parable of the prodigal son. In that story, when the son returns home, the father runs to him. Many scholars believe that this was considered shameful at that time. Respectable men did not run, especially to sons who had shamed the family. But there is no amount of shame the father won't endure to reconnect with his son. And there is no shame that God will not endure to reconnect with us. Jesus was shamed in both life and death to restore our relationship with God.

Have you ever thought about that? That you are so loved by God that he is willing to allow shame to come upon himself in order to reach you? That you matter that much to the Lord?

Though they don't always realize it, this is the reason the disciples have sacrificed so much to be with Jesus. They have left everything behind to follow the One who left everything behind for them. They are modeling the behavior of their rabbi from the very moment they join him.

Perhaps this is why, decades later, the same John who was questioning Jesus earlier in this episode would himself write, "This is how God showed his love among us: He sent his one and only Son into the world that we might live through him. This is love: not that we loved God, but that he loved us and sent his Son as an atoning sacrifice for our sins" (1 John 4:9–10 NIV).

It is with his bold declaration of love that Jesus invites us all to be his disciples. The question that will linger throughout this episode, though, is how much people are willing to surrender to accept that invitation. Will they leave the life they have to accept the life that Jesus is offering?

Chapter 26

NOT MY SON

Family matters.

Throughout Scripture, we consistently see commands and accounts highlighting the value of family and its essential role in our relationship with the Lord. Families protect and provide for one another, pass down the faith to one another, and fight alongside one another. In fact, one of the worst punishments in Scripture is to be cast away from one's family and the people of God (see, e.g., Ex. 31:14; Lev. 7:20–21; Num. 15:30).

This explains the tragedy that surrounds Matthew the tax collector in episode 7: he has lost his family.

Early in the episode, Matthew returns to his family home in Capernaum. He is greeted at the door by his mother and she invites him inside, but their exchange quickly becomes awkward and unpleasant. He addresses her by her first name rather than calling her Eema (the Hebrew and Aramaic word for "mother"). She says that she could not even let him in the house if his father were present.

As their conversation continues, Matthew's mother laments his decision to become a tax collector. She accuses him of accepting "blood money" and says he has used his talents to "bleed [his] people dry."

Remember, tax collectors were despised in first-century Jewish culture. They were considered dishonest and corrupt, impoverishing their own people for the benefit of Rome and of themselves. By choosing this life, Matthew brought shame not only to himself but also to his entire family.

Why would he do this?

Matthew has been disowned by his family. In a culture where family was at the center of life, why would he be willing to make that sacrifice? What about tax collecting was so alluring that he would leave his entire family behind?

Well, at the time of Jesus, there were two primary types of tax collectors: *mokhes* (pronounced *mo-khes*) and *gabbai* (pronounced *gah-bye)*. Gabbai collected property, income, and poll taxes. These were generally set taxes with little room for interpretation. Mokhes, however, collected taxes on imports and exports, trade goods, and anything that was transported by road. They had great discretion and could easily cheat people. Whatever they collected above what they owed Rome, they could keep for themselves.[1]

We see this distinction in Greek, though in different terms. Matthew is referred to as a *telones*, whereas Zacchaeus is called an *architelones*.

As a mokhes, Matthew was seen as the worst type of tax collector. This is what his mother meant when she accused him of bleeding his people dry. He became rich while his family and neighbors became poor. This is why he would have been disowned by his family: he had turned his back on them, shamed them, and harmed his people.

Apparently for Matthew, the profit seemed worth the sacrifice. While he might have been leaving his family behind, he was also gaining things that had previously seemed unattainable: wealth and power.

He would be working alongside Rome rather than simply existing as a subject under their authority. While many around him were looking for a Messiah to come and rescue them, Matthew had found his own path of salvation, and he was determined to pave it himself.

But in Matthew's exchange with his mother, we also witness the confusion that he surely would have faced. He is wondering, *Why can't I have both? Why can't I have my family and retain my position? Why won't they see my point of view? Why won't they accept me and the decisions I have made?*

If we're honest, many of us struggle with these questions today, though perhaps in less extreme circumstances. Every day, we are bombarded with promises of happiness, freedom, and even salvation:

Buy this product!

Follow this leader!

Achieve this goal!

Do these things and your life will be all that you want it to be.

We are constantly told that we should take our own path, follow our own hearts, and be our own persons, despite what that might mean to those around us. We should be free and independent, and everyone else should support that. But every time, reality strikes, and we are faced with the same question Matthew faces: What am I willing to leave behind to pursue what I desire?

When we see someone like Matthew, our first response shouldn't be judgment; it should be humility. We too have been tempted. We too have given in.

The questions for Matthew—and for each of us—are: How long will I stay there? How long will I leave behind what I know matters most? And when Jesus does come along, will I be willing to abandon my own plans to pursue his?

Chapter 27

REBIRTHING PAINS

There are some moments from the life of Jesus that nearly every Christian would long to have witnessed in person: the feeding of the five thousand, the Sermon on the Mount, the resurrection, and more. If we are fans of *The Chosen*, we look forward to having some of those moments depicted for us.

One such moment occurs in episode 7. As Jesus sits to speak with Nicodemus, the events of John 3 unfold. Having seen and heard so much about Jesus, and filled with questions he simply cannot answer, Nicodemus seeks out Jesus himself.

At the heart of their conversation are two questions: Who is Jesus? and, What is he here to do?

These things are being asked not only by Nicodemus but also by other religious leaders, and even by Roman soldiers like Quintus. They are trying to determine what message Jesus is preaching and whether or not this message is a threat to their interests.

But for Nicodemus, these questions about Jesus' identity and message aren't so much focused on the things he wants to preserve; Nicodemus is focused on those things that he hopes will change. He is yearning for a spiritual revival among the people, and he hopes that Jesus might be the one who will bring it.

Now, of course, the storylines and conversations mentioned are from *The Chosen*'s script rather than from the actual biblical narrative. But they do highlight concerns that would have been present among religious leaders encountering Jesus at that time, perhaps even Nicodemus.

For instance, Nicodemus asks Jesus, "What have you come here to show us?" and Jesus replies, "A kingdom." Nicodemus then says, "That is what our rulers are worried about."

Through this statement, Nicodemus is underscoring the very real concerns of the Roman Empire. As we saw earlier, Rome's mission was to maintain control and order. Anyone who tried to establish his own kingdom within the empire would be a threat to that.

And yet, that is exactly what Jesus is trying to do. He may not be trying to build a physical kingdom, but his realm will be no less threatening. Jesus' mission is to usher in God's reign upon the earth. This inherently declares that it is not the emperor who truly rules or the local governor who is in power; it is the Lord whom people will follow and serve.

This is what Nicodemus hears Jesus saying when he says, "Very truly I tell you, no one can see the kingdom of God unless they are born again" (John 3:3 NIV). He's saying that people can have no other allegiances above their commitment to the Lord. They must leave behind their old lives and surrender their hearts to the Lord and to his Messiah.

And yet, Jesus' statement brings confusion. Nicodemus immediately responds, "How can someone be born when they are old? ... Surely they cannot enter a second time into their mother's womb to be born!" (v. 4 NIV).

The confusion comes from the Greek word *anōthen* (pronounced *an'-o-then*), which means both "from above" and "again." With this word, Jesus is communicating that the kingdom he is bringing is both spiritual and physical. To experience it, people must both experience spiritual rebirth and begin new lives. They must leave behind their past lives and begin new ones in which Jesus reigns both in their hearts and through their actions. This is the only way to experience God's reign on earth and in heaven.

Nicodemus helps us see the true challenge for people who are deciding whether to follow Jesus. There are risks to following Jesus. It involves danger and sacrifice.

If Nicodemus chooses to pursue Jesus' kingdom, to essentially become one of Jesus' disciples, he will face very real threats from Rome's kingdom. And if he chooses to embrace Jesus as Lord, he will face the wrath of those he calls brothers, his fellow religious leaders. He will have to surrender the power and stature he has worked so hard to achieve throughout his life.

This is not an easy decision. Jesus does not intend for it to be.

In fact, the closer we look at Jesus' words, the clearer his intentions become. Jesus isn't promising that if Nicodemus becomes a disciple of Jesus, it will be easy. He isn't pretending that there won't be consequences. Jesus is making it clear that to follow him, Nicodemus (or anyone considering such a life) will have to leave everything behind.

Just as Jesus' disciples have left their homes and families, all who want to follow Jesus (including Nicodemus) will need to walk away from their old lives to experience new life through him. Some things may stay the same. But in the end, there will be one fundamental difference: Jesus will be at the center of everything. Every thought, every decision, every act must stem from one's love for and devotion to Jesus.

This will bring unbelievable joy. But it will also come with costs. And the question before Nicodemus and each of us is: What am I willing to leave behind so that I might receive all that Jesus has to offer?

Chapter 28

THE TALE OF TWO RICH YOUNG MEN

Sometimes the paths our lives take come down to just a few decisions. If we hadn't applied for that job, attended that event, or left the house when we did, life as we know it might be entirely different.

My wife and I were reminiscing about this recently. We recalled the moment, before we were dating, when we were at a restaurant and I was planning to tell her how I truly felt about her. When the time came to pay the check, she stopped me from taking it and insisted, "No, thanks. I'll pay for myself."

I was stunned. Here I was, about to profess my feelings for her, and she wouldn't even let me pay for the meal!

Fortunately, though, I couldn't back out. That afternoon, I had told my friends at work what I was planning to do. There was no way I could return to work the next day if I didn't follow through with it. So, amid all the awkwardness, I told her how I felt about her.

We've been together ever since.

I often wonder what might have happened if I had chickened out that night. Would we have still gotten together? Would it have just taken longer to happen? Or would both of our lives have forever been different?

As episode 7 draws to a close, Matthew is faced with just such a dilemma. Still reeling from his recent conversation with his mother, he is confused and unsettled about the decisions he has made and the life he has chosen.

In that moment, Jesus appears. He stops as he's walking by with his disciples, looks directly at Matthew, and says something unthinkable. He addresses this tax collector, this despised man, this man who is so shameful that his own family has disowned him, and says, "Follow me."

As we have seen, this is no mere invitation for Matthew to join him for a stroll. Jesus is inviting Matthew to be his disciple. Even Simon, who himself would have been considered unworthy of any rabbi, is upset by this invitation. And ironically, so is Gaius the Roman soldier, who has become something of an unlikely friend to Matthew.

In Gaius's eyes, Matthew is abandoning everything that he himself considers valuable. Matthew has worked so hard and sacrificed so much to attain a position that others envy. Yet, in an instant, Matthew walks away from all of it. Gaius is left wondering, Who would do such a thing?

To appreciate this moment, it may help to look at a similar moment in Scripture. Several gospels record an encounter between Jesus and a man very much like Matthew. The man is rich and influential. But unlike Matthew, he is considered righteous.

As Luke tells it, the man approaches Jesus and asks how to inherit eternal life. Jesus responds, "You know the commandments: 'Do not commit adultery, do not murder, do not steal, do not give false testimony, honor your father and mother'" (18:20). The man replies that he has observed all of these commands since he was a youth.

Jesus then does something surprising. He tells the man that he lacks one thing: he must sell his possessions, give the money to the poor, and then come and follow him. Just like in the scene with Matthew, Jesus is inviting this rich man to be his disciple.

But the rich man simply cannot (or will not) do it.

Apparently, his possessions hold too much value. He cannot bear to part with them. He is unwilling to leave his old life behind in this way.

But Matthew isn't!

In both the Gospels and the episode, Matthew abandons his tax booth to follow Jesus. In doing so, he surrenders his investment, his position, and everything else he has worked for years to secure.

As Matthew does this, it leaves us wondering: What will Nicodemus do? He is another rich man who has much to lose by following Jesus. He, like Matthew, has power and influence. He has sacrificed so much to get where he is. Will the draw of the gospel, of the good news that Jesus is bringing, be compelling enough for Nicodemus? Or will his old life be too difficult to leave behind?

Even two thousand years later, we can't help but sense how ironic this situation is. The sinful tax collector abandoned everything immediately. All it took was Jesus' invitation. But for the righteous Pharisee, it's just not that simple.

In the end, Matthew's conversion reminds us that our external acts of righteousness are not always an accurate indicator of our faith in Jesus. Following Jesus is not a matter of how many rules we follow or how holy we appear in the eyes of those around us. Following Jesus is a question of what we are willing to surrender—what we will leave behind—to devote ourselves to him.

Remember, Jesus gave up everything for you, abandoned heaven to be with you. This is not a one-sided relationship. Rather, it is an invitation to enter into a relationship of mutual surrender.

> To each of us, Jesus says, "This is the relationship I want with you. Be bound to me. Give your heart to me as I have given myself for you."

When my wife and I got married, this is the vow we made to each other. My life is forever tied to hers, and hers to mine. We sacrifice for each other every day. But we do so not out of obligation or fear of reprisal. We do so out of love. Her joy is my joy; her path is my path; in prosperity and failure, we are forever bound to one another.

And I would have it no other way.

To each of us, Jesus says, "This is the relationship I want with you. Be bound to me. Give your heart to me as I have given myself for you."

The question is, Would we have it any other way?

Episode 8

SEEING

There is a design on the ceiling of our upstairs bathroom. It isn't intentional. This small spectrum of colors, which takes up about five square inches, is a combination of swirls and shapes, blues and pinks, yellows and oranges. It took only a day to create, but its presence is everlasting.

This design became a permanent feature of our home because one day my daughter came home from church with a balloon. It was her birthday, and her Sunday school teacher gave her a balloon to celebrate. She loved this balloon, and she took it with her everywhere in the house—even into the bathroom.

But one day, she forgot to take it out with her when she left, so the balloon stayed in the bathroom. It remained there for a day or so, resting gently on the ceiling above where we washed our faces, brushed our teeth, and took our showers.

Eventually, I decided the balloon needed to come down, so I removed it from the bathroom. But that wasn't the end of the matter. Left behind was a patch of ink that had seeped from the balloon onto the ceiling, probably when someone had taken a hot shower.

We tried everything to remove it, but nothing worked. Ultimately, we decided we could either repaint the entire ceiling or just learn to live with it. We chose the latter. And eventually, we stopped noticing the stain on our ceiling. We walk beneath it dozens of times each day, and it never catches our attention.

It is strange how our minds have the ability to do that, isn't it? To not see things?

They exist. We know they are there. But we do not see them.

But what happens when those "things" are actually people? People who exist, but we don't see them?

Or when they are realities about ourselves and our situations that are obvious to others but that we refuse to accept?

In a sermon to his hometown of Nazareth, Jesus proclaimed that he had come to fulfill God's promise to bring "recovery of sight to the blind" (Luke 4:18). He told them he had come to help people see. And in the final episode of season 1, we will see how this promise brings tremendous healing to those who don't even know they're blind.

Chapter 29

THE GOD WHO SEES

The Bible is filled with insiders and outsiders. The insiders are those who are part of God's people, the central figures in Scripture from whom we glean understanding about our own relationships with the Lord. Abraham, Moses, Ruth, and Mary are just a few of those who receive special attention.

But what about the outsiders, those who are not part of God's people? What about the kings of foreign nations? Or the Gentiles encountered by the prophets (such as the people of Nineveh whom Jonah preached to or the Gentile widow and her son whom Elijah encountered during the drought)? What about those who live along the periphery of God's chosen people?

One such outsider is Hagar. She was the Egyptian slave woman who bore Abraham's first son. For a while, she was the mother of his only heir. Nevertheless, most people today think of her as secondary, a false replacement for his true wife, Sarah.

In many ways, this is how Hagar's story unfolds in Scripture as well (read Hagar's story in Genesis 16 and 21). Even though it was Sarah's idea to give Hagar to Abraham to bear a child, when Hagar became pregnant, there was enmity between Hagar and Sarah. Ishmael's birth caused an imbalance in their relationship, elevating Hagar (a slave) over Abraham's own wife. Sarah became furious with the way Hagar was treating her, so she began to abuse Hagar, and Abraham did nothing to stop it.

While this might seem unjust to us, it would have been considered entirely acceptable in the ancient Near East. Hagar was a slave; she was considered property. Sarah was permitted to do whatever she wanted to her.

What is uncommon, though, is God's treatment of Hagar.

After deciding that it was better to die in the wilderness than to endure more suffering, Hagar fled with her unborn son into the desert to escape Sarah's abuse. While she was there, though, the angel of the Lord appeared to her. He told her that she must return to Sarah and promised that God would bless her by producing many offspring through her.

In response to this gracious promise, Hagar responds, "'You are El-roi,' for she said, 'In this place, have I actually seen the one who sees me?'" (Gen. 16:13 CSB).

Early in episode 8, Nicodemus and his wife discuss this moment in Scripture. He comments that Hagar was caught up in a situation that was not of her choosing and that God knew the path she would have to take would not be an easy one.

These comments reflect the wrestling going on within Nicodemus's own soul. He has begun to see Jesus for who he truly is: God's Messiah. But simply seeing things as they are does not mean that one can always see the path forward. Nicodemus cannot imagine how he could follow Jesus while also maintaining the life he has worked so hard to build.

In many ways, Nicodemus reflects the struggle we all face when confronted with the gospel. Jesus himself says, "If anyone would come after me, let him deny himself and take up his cross and follow me. For whoever would save his life will lose it, but whoever loses his life for my sake will find it" (Matt. 16:24–25 ESV). As we have seen, being a disciple wasn't simply a matter of acknowledging the greatness of the rabbi—it was also a decision to surrender everything to follow him.

> Following Jesus is not easy, but it is worth every step, because the future we have with him is far greater than any future we could ever have on our own. His promise is not just some distant hope of salvation once our journey is over; it is an assurance that he will be with us all along the way.

For us, this is the difference between simply saying "I believe in Jesus" and truly giving our lives to him. It is the difference between attending church on Sunday and actually letting Jesus be the Lord and Savior of every part of our lives.

The truth is that following Jesus will cost us. We will have to give up things. We will need to make changes in our lives. We will have to surrender our priorities for his priorities, our desires for his desires. And sometimes, that cost might seem too great and the path might seem too hard.

But this is where the words of Hagar give us hope. Just as God saw her in her moment of despair and confusion, God sees us when we are concerned about the cost of following Jesus. Just as the angel of the

Lord promised Hagar a greater future on the other side of her difficult journey, so Jesus promises the same to us.

Following Jesus is not easy, but it is worth every step, because the future we have with him is far greater than any future we could ever have on our own. His promise is not just some distant hope of salvation once our journey is over; it is an assurance that he will be with us all along the way.

Perhaps you have been praying to the Lord for quite some time but have heard nothing in response.

Perhaps your faith in Jesus has cost you your friends. Or your job. Or your dreams.

Perhaps you find yourself paralyzed in your relationship with the Lord, wanting to move forward but still consumed by the temptation to hold something back from him.

If this is where you find yourself, I want you to hear these words ... God sees you.

That may be hard to sense or even to accept. You may have many reasons to feel otherwise. But I want you to know that you are not alone. God not only sees you; he is with you.

This is the power of the cross. Jesus is proof that we have a God who does not just watch us from the shadows; he enters into the darkness with us.

More than that, we have a God who brings the light. For in your darkest moment, Jesus does not just see you; he gives you the ability to see. To see that there is hope. To see that you are loved. And to see the salvation that only he can offer, the gift that is worth surrendering everything to receive.

Chapter 30

UNSAVORY DINNER GUESTS

What do you do when your life is transformed for the better? Like when you get married? Or when you find out that you are pregnant? Or when you discover that you possess the winning lottery ticket?

Odds are, you throw a party. When great things happen to us, our natural desire is to share that joy with others.

It is no surprise, then, that upon becoming a disciple of Jesus, Matthew hosts a feast to celebrate this incredible change in his life. He invites Jesus, the other disciples, and—most curiously—other tax collectors.

It makes sense that Matthew would have had friends who were also tax collectors. But it is surprising that he invites them to dine with Jesus, a respected rabbi. And it is even more surprising that Jesus attends.

At this time in Israel, people worked hard to be seen in a favorable light by those with power and influence in the community. They were careful about who they were seen with. You were judged not only by the life you lived but also by the company you kept.

Matthew knows that he risks bringing shame to his new rabbi; so does Jesus. Probably every other rabbi of that day would avoid being associated with even one tax collector, let alone a whole group of them. Yet Jesus chooses to be seen at this table surrounded by this crowd. To understand why, we have to look at what Jesus says when he is confronted about this situation during the dinner: "The Pharisees and their scribes began grumbling to His disciples, saying, 'Why do you eat and drink with the tax collectors and sinners?' And Jesus answered and said to them, 'It is not those who are healthy who need a physician, but those who are sick. I have not come to call the righteous to repentance, but sinners'" (Luke 5:30–32 NASB).

In Galilee at this time, a meal like this was a public event. Even people who were not invited to the dinner would sometimes watch from the outside.[1] This is why the Pharisees were present.

But while a large dinner may have been a public spectacle, it was also a very intimate experience. Sharing a meal with someone was seen as an act of acceptance. And since there is no evidence that the other tax collectors at this meal have had the same transformative experience that Matthew had, the Pharisees are concerned that Jesus is accepting of their sins. They don't have an issue with the fact that Jesus may call these sinners to repent. Their concern is that this didn't happen before he chose to dine with them.[2]

> This is the hope of the gospel: Jesus accepts us for who we are, right where we are. He does not demand that we become sinless before we approach him. He says, "Approach, and I will heal you of your sin."

But Jesus' response to the Pharisees communicates something deeper than a call for sinners to repent. It reveals how he sees sinners (and sin itself) in the first place. He does not see sinners just as those who break the law. He sees them as beloved children of God sickened by the sin in their lives and in desperate need of healing. And Jesus is uniquely suited to provide this.

The Greek word that we translate *Jesus* is actually the word *Iēsous*, the Greek transliteration of the Hebrew word *Yeshua*. This would have been the actual name Jesus received at birth, the name with which he would have been addressed throughout the entire Jewish community.

As with all Jewish names, Yeshua was a name that held meaning. It means "God saves." Jesus' very name declares his purpose: he has come to "save his people from their sins" (Matt. 1:21).

Here too the true meaning is lost in English. In Greek, the word translated "to save" is the word *sozo (pronounced sode'-zo)*. But sozo can also mean "to heal."

Suddenly, Jesus' response to the Pharisees takes on new meaning. These men are sick, trapped in their sin and the lives they have chosen. And he has come not only to save them from their sins but also to heal them, to transform their very hearts.

In a world where religious leaders like the Pharisees put up barriers to block these tax collectors from associating with others, Jesus does the opposite. He reveals that true healing will come not through a stricter adherence to the law but through a deeper relationship with him.

This is the hope of the gospel: Jesus accepts us for who we are, right where we are. He does not demand that we become sinless before we approach him. He says, "Approach, and I will heal you of your sin."

This is the promise of salvation: not just that we can be forgiven, but that we will be changed. Jesus sees into our very natures, peering even into those shameful places we do not want to be seen, and he helps us to see beyond who we are to who we can become through him.

This is what Matthew realized that led him to leave his tax booth that day. It may even be the reason he invited his fellow tax collectors to dinner that night. And it is what Jesus is trying to help each and every one of us to see as well.

Chapter 31

CONFLICT BETWEEN COUSINS

When I was fifteen, I decided to grow long sideburns. This trend was returning from its former glory in the 1960s and '70s and was sweeping through my high school. I thought I would gain lots of respect because at fifteen I had no trouble growing nice, long, thick sideburns.

Unfortunately for me, they were atrocious! They looked like two fat caterpillars on my face. For two years, I did not go on one date, and I just knew it was all thanks to those sideburns. (Though this doesn't explain why I couldn't get a date for the next two years after I shaved them off.)

What still baffles me, though, is why, for those two long years, I never shaved them. I sensed that they were not attractive. Some people even had the courage (or perhaps cruelty) to tell me they weren't attractive. Nevertheless, I allowed them to remain.

In many ways, it was as if I did not want to see them. I did not want to admit how bad they looked. I essentially convinced myself that if I kept the sideburns, either their appearance would improve or others' opinions of them would.

Perhaps this is a natural human defense mechanism: we choose to not see that which might cause us pain or embarrassment. It was certainly the case for many at the time of Jesus.

Partway through episode 8, Jesus and his disciples begin a journey south. Eventually, they come to a crossroads where they must decide whether they are going to travel through—or go around—a region called Samaria.

Typically, Jews would do the latter. Samaria could be a dangerous area, rife with thieves. But Jews had another reason: They simply didn't want to see it. They didn't want to be anywhere near the people who lived there.

This attitude came from a long-standing conflict between Jews and Samaritans that dated back to the Assyrian exile. Second Kings 17 tells the story of how, when Assyria conquered Israel, many people were forcibly removed from Israel and sent elsewhere in the Assyrian Empire. Meanwhile, Assyria brought in other conquered people to replace the Israelites they had removed. Eventually, those Jews who remained in Israel intermarried with Gentiles who had been brought in, and the generations that followed became the "half-breed" Samaritans.

More than a century later, the rest of the Jews (those living in the southern kingdom, called Judah) were conquered by Babylonia, and many were taken there into exile. After seventy years of exile, many Jews returned to Israel from Babylonian captivity, and they began to fight with the Samaritans. They considered the Samaritans to be outsiders, not fully Jewish. This ultimately led to a rift so great that Samaritans had to build their own temple (at Mount Gerizim) because they were prohibited from worshipping in the Jerusalem temple. Samaritans were designated *am ha-aretz*, which means "unclean."[1]

It is the same word used to describe lepers.

Jewish children were raised to hate Samaritans, and Samaritans were raised to hate Jews. Jesus' own disciples display this hatred. At one point, when messengers whom Jesus has sent to Samaria are rejected, James and John ask, "Lord, do you want us to call fire to come down from heaven and consume them?" (Luke 9:54). Their hatred runs so deep that they want to completely wipe them out.

As far as Jesus' disciples are concerned, it is better to simply avoid Samaritans. If they do not have to see them, things will be better for both parties. But just as Jesus is the God who sees us, he is also the One who teaches us to see one another.

Jesus rejects the hatred that his disciples feel for Samaritans. He intentionally takes his disciples to see the very people they despise. It is Jesus' way of showing them that his kingdom has no place for hatred. If they are to be his disciples, his reflection in this world, then they must see others as he sees them.

Can I ask you: Who is it that you need to *see*? Whom do you try to avoid? Where is there a barrier between you and those Jesus is calling you to serve?

One of the biggest challenges in our relationship with Jesus is that we are often asked to offer healing to others while still being in need of healing ourselves. We are called to share a gospel that is still unfolding in our own lives. We are imperfect people reaching out to imperfect people.

So were Jesus' disciples.

The twelve men following Jesus were not spotless saints, free from all sin. They struggled. They doubted. They sinned. And at times, they were even rebuked by Jesus. Nevertheless, they followed. Despite their fears and frustrations, they listened to their rabbi and went wherever he led.

Jesus expects the same from us. He doesn't require us to be holy and righteous throughout our journey with him. He simply asks that we keep following. Keep listening. Keep surrendering. He will take care of the rest.

Chapter 32

AN AWKWARD TRANSFORMATION

In the middle of an open field, Jesus sits down next to an ancient well. This well has a history. It was believed that, centuries earlier, Jacob had dug this very well after buying the land from the sons of Hamor (see Gen. 33:19; John 4:5–6). So, in the middle of the day, Jesus sits beside this well, waiting for a certain someone to come along and draw water for him. That person doesn't know it yet, but Jesus is here for a divine appointment.

Eventually, a woman approaches. In the eyes of people at the time, this would be an improper encounter for several reasons. First, this woman is alone, and it was not appropriate for any man, especially a religious leader like Jesus, to be alone with a woman. Their meeting could have spawned rumors and brought shame upon them both.

Second, the encounter would seem awkward because there is a reason this woman comes alone. Typically, women would collect water in groups. It was a social event. They would do this early in the morning to avoid being outside in the warmer parts of the day.[1]

But this woman comes to the well both alone and in the middle of the day. It appears she may not be welcome with the other women of her community. Not only is Jesus alone with a woman; he is alone with a shunned woman—possibly one of ill repute.

Then of course there is the fact that this woman is a Samaritan. As we have seen, she and her people were despised by Jews. From the perspective of the customs and scruples of the day, there is no reason for Jesus to be anywhere near this woman.

Everything about this situation appears wrong. And yet, as the scene unfolds, it becomes clear that this moment is about something more than the meeting of two people at a well; it is about things unseen.

After the woman balks at Jesus' request for her to draw him water from the well, he says, "If you had known the gift of God and who it is who says to you, 'Give me water to drink,' you would have asked him, and he would have given you living water" (John 4:10). Upon hearing the words *living water*, the woman would probably have assumed that Jesus had access to a river or stream. *Living water* was a term used to describe flowing water, unlike that found in ponds and cisterns. But as usual, Jesus is speaking of deeper things.

Jesus promises her, "Whoever drinks of this water which I will give to him will never be thirsty for eternity, but the water which I will give to him will become in him a well of water springing up to eternal life" (v. 14). This situation isn't about his physical thirst; it is about her spiritual thirst. It is about a thirst that cannot easily be identified.

Jesus reveals the source of her thirst—something he should not be able to know, having never met her. He exposes the pain of her marital situation, that she has had five husbands and that the man she is with now is not her husband. This could mean that she has been divorced multiple times, or it could be that each of her previous husbands has died. Either way, this is the source of her pain. It has brought her shame and causes her to be excluded from society.

And Jesus sees it. He sees her.

But in seeing her, Jesus does something even greater: He frees her. He brings to light that which was hidden, that which was tucked away. His light shines on her darkness, and the darkness cannot overcome it.

Just like Hagar, just like the tax collectors, the Samaritan woman recognizes Adonai El-Roi: the God who sees. Now that this woman knows Jesus has seen her for who she is, she can see him for who he truly is. When she says, "I know that Messiah is coming," she is ready to believe him when Jesus responds, "I, the one speaking to you, am he" (vv. 25–26).

Indeed, this truth is so apparent to her that she abandons her shame, ignores the judgment of those in her community, and rushes back to town to tell her story to everyone who will listen (vv. 28–29). Now she can finally believe what was once unfathomable: there is hope for her. She can see it.

This moment is the culmination of everything that has been happening for eight episodes. God has come to earth, the ministry of the Messiah has begun, and people are beginning to see what it all means. Just as this woman's life is completely changed by Jesus' presence, so too will the entire world be changed.

Jesus is proof that God sees our suffering and our sin. He does not merely witness these things; he experiences them. And he allows us to see that there is hope.

We can be made new. We can be transformed. He is the One who will make those things possible.

If that is a hope that you long to experience, you don't have to wait. The offer is always there. You simply have to accept it.

So, if you'd like to accept this beautiful gift of God's grace, then I'd like to join with you as you surrender your heart to him and plead with him to give you new life. And if you gave your life to Jesus a long time ago, then may this be an opportunity for me to pray for your continuing journey with Jesus, asking God to sustain you, no matter what life might bring.

Let's pray.

> Jesus, I thank you for the beautiful gift of your gospel, of this good news that we read about in Scripture and experience in our lives. I thank you for this journey that we are taking together, watching it unfold around us every day, and in shows like *The Chosen*.

> I lift up the one who is praying with me right now, especially the one who is longing to experience new life through you. Make this person new, Lord. Remove the chains that bind them. Heal their wounds. Wipe away their sin. Set them free!

> Help us, Jesus, to choose you each and every day. To surrender everything to you. To give our lives for you, just as you gave your life for us. And to know that the life you offer is greater than any life we could choose for ourselves.

> We need your strength to do this, Lord. So, may you fill us with your presence for the rest of our days and surround us with your Spirit. And each day, may we

witness how we are drawn closer to you, ever deeper into a relationship that is greater than any we could ask for or deserve.

We surrender our hearts to you, Jesus. And we thank you for your love.

It is in the strength of your name that we pray! Amen.

Conclusion

WHAT'S NEXT?

A s we journey through the life and teachings of Jesus, we find truths revealed therein that impact every phase of our own journey. And as we learn about the Lord, we can draw closer to him. The goal is not for us to reach a static point, a moment when we say, "This is as far as I need to go." The goal is to keep going, keep searching, keep discovering, and keep growing.

In the eight episodes of season 1 of *The Chosen*, we have discovered many things about Jesus. Hopefully, we have been changed by them. But just as the series is far from its end, so too is our journey through the Bible.

Jesus isn't inviting us to reach a destination. He is inviting us into an ongoing relationship. He is saying, "Let me be your Savior each and every day. Follow me and be my disciple."

We have watched as people have surrendered their lives for this, left their families, abandoned their possessions. They knew the sacrifice they were making, but they made it gladly because they also knew the treasure they were attaining.

As Jesus says in Matthew's gospel, "The kingdom of heaven is like treasure hidden in a field. When a man found it, he hid it again, and then in his joy went and sold all he had and bought that field. Again, the kingdom of heaven is like a merchant looking for fine pearls. When he found one of great value, he went away and sold everything he had and bought it" (13:44–46 NIV).

The kingdom of heaven awaits us. And as we have seen, this isn't just a promise of some future glory; this is a very real and present hope. The work begun in the Gospels is still unfolding around us.

The question is: Will we join Jesus on this journey? And what are we willing to give up to do so?

Jesus isn't inviting us to reach a destination. He is inviting us into an ongoing relationship. He is saying, "Let me be your Savior each and every day. Follow me and be my disciple."

If you're honest, you may find that you don't yet have good answers to those questions. Like many in *The Chosen*, you may still be at an early point in your relationship with Jesus; much of your story has yet to unfold.

Nevertheless, to find those answers, you must keep exploring, questioning, and discerning who Jesus is and what all of this means. So, as you reach the end of this book, I want to offer you a few challenges:

First, rewatch season 1 of *The Chosen*. How will knowing what you know now, because of this book, cause you to view the episodes differently? What will you notice that you never saw before? How will this change the way you understand the show and the overall gospel message? Write down your observations.

Next, read through the first four to five chapters of each gospel. This will cover the bulk of what has happened in the first season of *The Chosen*. Note the similarities and differences between the show and Scripture. Then reflect on how the insights you've learned in this book have changed the

way you read those Scriptures. What new things
do you notice? What looks different now?

Finally, discuss both of these things with other
people. Jewish culture was highly communal.
There were even certain prayers that could
not be spoken without a minimum number of
participants.[1] We can learn on our own. But we
learn better with others. Share a copy of this book
with a friend. Then allow God to work through
your conversations to bring you both even more
insights than you uncovered by yourselves.

As I said in the preface, my goal has been to help you appreciate
The Chosen in a whole new way and encourage you to hunger even
more for God's Word. I hope that you can now watch the show with
new eyes, seeing and enjoying things that you previously missed. But
more important, I hope that you can now view Scripture with a new
set of eyes.

Insights like the rabbi–disciple relationship, the Jewish education
system, and the messianic expectations of the first century allow us
to do something that not even *The Chosen* can accomplish: immerse
ourselves in the world of Scripture.

Now, you might say that this is exactly what *The Chosen* does.
It has given us the ability to imagine the world of Jesus in a whole
new way, and ourselves in it. We connect with the disciples and their
experiences. We get to see the first-century Jewish context depicted in
uniquely accurate ways. All of this is true.

But in the end, one thing remains true: *The Chosen* is not the Bible. It is a television show—and a really good one, at that. As you've seen over the past thirty-two chapters, sometimes the show changes things or adds things that are not in the Bible. And even though it usually gets more right than wrong, it still isn't Scripture.

You are now equipped with knowledge and insights that can do much more than help you enjoy a television show; they can open the world of the Bible to you in beautiful new ways.

For instance, whenever you're reading in the Gospels the story of Jesus calling Simon to follow him, you may smile as you remember the scene from episode 4, when Simon's boat is overflowing with fish and he falls at Jesus' feet. Having read this book, you now know that this moment is special not because of a fictional story about overdue taxes. It's remarkable because Simon abandons everything and surrenders his life to Jesus. Now you know that as far back as he can remember, he has been told he isn't good enough to follow a rabbi. He has come to terms with the fact that he would spend the rest of his life continuing his father's trade.

But suddenly, everything is different. Not only does he have the opportunity to follow a rabbi, but his rabbi is the Messiah.

And with that, this familiar story takes on an entirely new dimension. The Holy Spirit speaks to you in a way unlike ever before. You start to recognize the places in your life where people gave up on you—perhaps where you even gave up on yourself—but now you can hear that Jesus is saying, "Come. Follow me. I choose you."

Ultimately, this is the goal of *The Chosen*: not to make you fall in love with a television show that could someday be forgotten, but to draw you into the Word of God, which is eternal and unchanging.

My hope is that this book has also drawn you deeper into the Word of God, that it has opened a door through which the Holy Spirit can speak into your life. I hope it has lit a fire in your heart, such that you can't wait to read the Bible each day.

Do you want to know something amazing? This is just the beginning of the incredible journey God has in store for you, one that will draw you ever closer to the Lord and ever deeper into the Bible.

Thank you for allowing me to be part of that journey! And I can't wait to see what God has in store for us next!

* Be on the lookout for *The Forgotten Teachings of Jesus: Rediscovering the Bible with The Chosen: Season 2*, where we continue our journey through the Bible as we examine ways the episodes in season 2 intersect with Scripture and how they reflect life in Israel at the time of Jesus.

ACKNOWLEDGMENTS

There are some things in life that you imagine but never truly believe you will get to do.

For much of my life, I have thought about writing books, imagining what it would be like to one day be an author. I still have a hard time believing that those dreams have become reality.

One thing I know for certain, though, is that I have not reached this place alone. The work of this book and the impact God has made through me over the past few years have only been possible because of the love, support, and efforts of so many people in my life.

First and foremost, I thank the Lord for the doors that have opened and the gift that this ministry has become in my life. I believe the good news of Jesus is the greatest message that anyone can hear, and I am honored to be able to share it. It is he who deserves all the praise!

I would also like to thank my wife for all of her support, both while I have been working on this book and since my ministry began. Many times, she has seen me sitting in front of the computer late at night, working on a chapter or editing a video. She has stood by my side both in moments of elation and times of frustration. Never has she wavered. LeeAnn, I cherish you. And I couldn't do this without you.

To my beautiful daughters: You are the greatest gift that God has ever given me and your mother. Everything else could disappear tomorrow, but our lives would still be filled with joy because we have you. Thank you for the cuddles on a hard day that wipe away the stress of work, the invitations to play that remind me never to get lost in a task, and for simply bringing such joy and love into our lives.

To my parents and my sister: There is not a day that goes by that I don't appreciate the love, support, and strength of our family. Dad, your work ethic and the balance you always found between work and family guide me each and every day. Mom, your genuine love for others is my constant reminder to make sure that my focus is always on people, not on projects. And Brittany, you have a gift for encouragement. On the hard days, your words are the inspiration I need to keep pushing and to never forget what this is all about.

To my extended family: Without you, I would not know Jesus. From the Bible stories you would tell me as a child to your consistent presence in church, you helped establish the foundation of my faith. Everything God has done since has been a result of the work God did through you so early on. You have made this ministry possible in ways you will never know.

To my church: Thank you for the honor of being your pastor. You bring Scripture to life, showing so many what it looks like to be the body of Christ. Through you, our community knows what it is to be loved by Jesus and invited into a relationship with him. You are truly people who care about people, and I look forward to the work God has yet to do through us.

NOTES

Chapter 1

1. Ann Spangler and Lois Tverberg, *Sitting at the Feet of Rabbi Jesus: How the Jewishness of Jesus Can Transform Your Faith* (Grand Rapids, MI: Zondervan, 2018), 189, Kindle.

2. Lois Tverberg, *Walking in the Dust of Rabbi Jesus: How the Jewish Words of Jesus Can Change Your Life* (Grand Rapids: MI: Zondervan, 2012), 148–49.

3. Spangler and Tverberg, *Sitting at the Feet of Rabbi Jesus*, 156.

Chapter 2

1. Ann Spangler and Lois Tverberg, *Sitting at the Feet of Rabbi Jesus: How the Jewishness of Jesus Can Transform Your Faith* (Grand Rapids, MI: Zondervan, 2018), 28, Kindle.

2. Ray Vander Laan, *Life and Ministry of the Messiah Discovery Guide: Learning the Faith of Jesus* (Grand Rapids, MI: Zondervan, 1999, 2009), 141.

3. Mark J. Keown, *Discovering the New Testament: An Introduction to Its Background, Theology, and Themes*, vol. 1, The Gospels and Acts (Bellingham, WA: Lexham, 2018), 187–88.

4. D. M. Edwards, "Ananias," in The International Standard Bible Encyclopedia, ed. Geoffrey W. Bromiley, rev. ed. (Grand Rapids, MI: Eerdmans, 1979–1988), 121.

Chapter 3

1. Thomas E. Schmidt, "Taxation, Jewish," *Dictionary of New Testament Background: A Compendium of Contemporary Biblical Scholarship* (Downers Grove, IL: InterVarsity Press, 2000), 1165.

Chapter 4

1. R. Riesner, "Archeology and Geography," in Dictionary of Jesus and the Gospels, eds. Joel B. Green, Jeannine K. Brown, and Nicholas Perrin, 2nd ed. (Downers Grove, IL: IVP Academic, 2013), 49.

2. Avraham Negev, *The Archaeological Encyclopedia of the Holy Land* (New York: Prentice Hall, 1990).

Chapter 7

1. Lavinia and Dan Cohn-Sherbok, A Popular Dictionary of Judaism (London: Taylor & Francis, 2013), 17.

Chapter 8

1. Mary's prayer appears to be drawn from a few Jewish sources. A typical Shabbat kiddush can be found at "Friday Night Kiddush (Hebrew/English Prayer PDF)," Chabad.org, accessed April 17, 2024, www.chabad.org/library/article_cdo/aid/258903/jewish/Friday-Night-Kiddush.htm.

Chapter 9

1. See Ann Spangler and Lois Tverberg, *Sitting at the Feet of Rabbi Jesus: How the Jewishness of Jesus Can Transform Your Faith* (Grand Rapids, MI: Zondervan, 2018), 28, Kindle.

Chapter 10

1. Lois Tverberg, *Walking in the Dust of Rabbi Jesus: How the Jewish Words of Jesus Can Change Your Life* (Grand Rapids: MI: Zondervan, 2012), 44, Kindle.

2. R. Alan Culpepper, "The Gospel of Luke," in *New Interpreter's Bible*, ed. Leander E. Keck, vol. 9 (Nashville: Abingdon, 1994–2004), 292.

3. David Bivin and Roy Blizzard Jr., Understanding the Difficult Words of Jesus: New Insights from a Hebraic Perspective, rev. ed. (Shippensburg, PA: Destiny Image, 1994).

Chapter 11

1. For Simon of Perea, see Josephus, Flavius. *Flavius Josephus: The Complete Works of Flavius Josephus* (Illustrated) . Kindle Edition. s, 17.273.

Chapter 12

1. Ann Spangler and Lois Tverberg, *Sitting at the Feet of Rabbi Jesus: How the Jewishness of Jesus Can Transform Your Faith* (Grand Rapids, MI: Zondervan, 2018), 16, Kindle.

Chapter 13

1. J. Carl Laney, "Fishing the Sea of Galilee," in *Lexham Geographic Commentary* on the Gospels, eds. Barry J. Beitzel and Kristopher A. Lyle, *Lexham Geographic Commentary* (Bellingham, WA: Lexham, 2016), 168–69.

2. Vernon H. Alexander, "The Words and Teachings of Jesus in the Context of Galilee," in Beitzel and Lyle, *Lexham Geographic Commentary on the Gospels*, 139.

Chapter 18

1. Ronald L. Eisenberg, The JPS Guide to Jewish Traditions (Philadelphia: Jewish Publication Society, 2004), 670.

2. Jacob Neusner, *The Mishnah: A New Translation* (New Haven, CT: Yale University Press, 1988), 678–679.

Chapter 20

1. Paul P. Enns, "Weddings," in *Holman Illustrated Bible Dictionary*, eds. Chad Brand et al. (Nashville: Holman Bible Publishers, 2003), 1664.

Chapter 21

1. Dennis M. Swanson, "Centurion," in *Eerdmans Dictionary of the Bible*, eds. David Noel Freedman, Allen C. Myers, and Astrid B. Beck (Grand Rapids, MI: Eerdmans, 2000), 228.

Chapter 22

1. Walter A. Elwell, ed., "Cleanness and Uncleanness, Regulations Concerning," *Baker Encyclopedia of the Bible* (Grand Rapids, MI: Baker Book House, 1988), 1:479.

Chapter 24

1. Ann Spangler and Lois Tverberg, *Sitting at the Feet of Rabbi Jesus: How the Jewishness of Jesus Can Transform Your Faith* (Grand Rapids, MI: Zondervan, 2018), 52, Kindle.

Chapter 25

1. Ann Spangler and Lois Tverberg, *Sitting at the Feet of Rabbi Jesus: How the Jewishness of Jesus Can Transform Your Faith* (Grand Rapids, MI: Zondervan, 2018), 31–32, Kindle.

2. Lois Tverberg, "The Reality of Disciples and Rabbis," Our Rabbi Jesus: Insights from Lois Tverberg (blog), September 16, 2023, ourrabbijesus. com/a-question-about-disciples-rabbis/.

Chapter 26

1. Alfred Edersheim, *The Life and Times of Jesus the Messiah* (New York: Longmans, Green, 1917), 515–18; and Alfred Plummer, *A Critical and Exegetical Commentary on the Gospel according to St. Luke*, International Critical Commentary (London: T&T Clark International, 1896), 159.

Chapter 30

1. Leander E. Keck, *New Interpreter's Bible*, vol. 9, *Luke, John* (Nashville: Abingdon, 1995), Luke 5:27–32 commentary, 127–28.

2. Keck, 128.

Chapter 31

1. Mishnah, Berakhot 47b:4-5, www.sefaria.org/sheets/371403?lang=bi, accessed August 28, 2024

Chapter 32

1. John D. Barry et al., *Faithlife Study Bible* (Bellingham, WA: Lexham, 2012, 2016), John 4:7.

Conclusion

1. Ann Spangler and Lois Tverberg, *Sitting at the Feet of Rabbi Jesus: How the Jewishness of Jesus Can Transform Your Faith* (Grand Rapids, MI: Zondervan, 2018), 267, Kindle.

Free Bonus Resources